PHP MySQL Cheat Sheet

(Cover all Basic PHP MySQL Syntaxes,
More Than 300 Examples)

Ray Yao

About This Book

This book covers all basic PHP syntaxes, almost each syntax entry lists a program example and result output. We can quickly reference the most helpful programming syntaxes, such as common command syntax, string function syntax, collection function syntax, class & object syntax......; all these syntaxes are very useful for programming.

We can take this book as a basic syntax manual because its entries are arranged alphabetically so that we can easily reference the important syntax.

This book also includes the basic MySQL syntax related to the PHP. Nowadays or in the future, the PHP Syntax Book can provide great help for coding both in our study and our work.

Disclaimer

This book is intended as a basic syntax manual only; it cannot include all entries on this subject. Its purpose is as a supplement for a cheat sheet book, not as a whole PHP dictionary.

Copyright © 2015 by Ray Yao's Team
All Rights Reserved

Neither part of this book nor whole of this book may be reproduced or transmitted in any form or by any means electronic, photographic or mechanical, including photocopying, recording, or by any information storage or retrieval system, without prior written permission from the author. All rights reserved!

Ray Yao's Team

Table of Contents

Syntax Chart 16

<!-- --> syntax: 16

__call() syntax: 16

__callstatic() syntax: 16

__construct() syntax: 17

__destruct() syntax: 17

$_COOKIE[ ] syntax: 18

$_ENV syntax: 19

$_FILE syntax: 19

$_GET[ ] syntax: 20

$_POST[ ] syntax: 20

$_REQUEST[ ] syntax: 21

$_SERVER[ ] syntax: 21

$_SERVER["REQUEST_METHOD"] syntax: 22

$_SESSION[ ] syntax: 22

$_SERVER['PHP_SELF'] syntax: 23

$GLOBALS syntax: 23

$PHP_SELF syntax: 24

$this syntax: 24

=> syntax: 25

== syntax: 25

=== syntax: 25

++$var and $var++ syntax: 25

--$var and $var-- syntax: 26

? : operator syntax: 26

<=> syntax: 26

__class__ syntax: 27

__dir__ syntax: 27

__file__ syntax: 27

__function__ syntax: 27

3

__line__ syntax: 28

__method__ syntax: 28

__namespace__ syntax: 28

__trait__ syntax: 28

abs() syntax: 29

abstract syntax: 29

addslashes() syntax: 30

alter table syntax: 30

alter table syntax: 31

arithmetical operator syntax: 32

array_change_key_case() syntax: 32

array_chunk() syntax: 33

array_combine() syntax: 33

array_count_values() syntax: 33

array creating syntax: 34

array creating syntax: 34

array_diff() syntax: 34

array_diff_assoc() syntax: 34

array_diff_key() syntax: 35

array_fill() syntax: 35

array_fill_keys() syntax: 35

array_flip() syntax: 36

array_intersect() syntax: 36

array_intersect_assoc() syntax: 36

array_intersect_key() syntax: 37

array_keys() syntax: 37

array_key_exists() syntax: 37

array_merge() syntax: 37

array_multisort($arr) syntax: 38

array_pad() syntax: 38

array_pop() syntax: 38

array_product() syntax: 38

array_push() syntax: 39

array_rand() syntax: 39

- array_reverse() syntax: 39
- array_search() syntax: 39
- array_shift() syntax: 40
- array size syntax: 40
- array_slice() syntax: 40
- array_splice() syntax: 41
- array_sum() syntax: 41
- array_unique() syntax: 41
- array_unshift() syntax: 41
- array_values() syntax: 42
- arsort() syntax: 42
- asort() syntax: 42
- assignment syntax: 43
- between…and… syntax: 43
- break statement syntax: 44
- ceil() syntax: 44
- checkbox input syntax: 44
- chdir() syntax: 45
- checkdate() syntax: 46
- chmod() syntax: 46
- chop() syntax: 46
- chr() syntax: 47
- chunk_split() syntax: 47
- class definition syntax: 47
- Class::method() syntax: 48
- clearstatcache(); 48
- close connection syntax: 49
- comment syntax: 49
- compact() syntax: 49
- conditional operator syntax: 50
- connect MySQL syntax: 50
- connect_error() syntax: 50
- const syntax: 51
- constant() syntax: 51

- constructor syntax: 51
- continue statement syntax: 52
- copy() syntax: 52
- count() syntax: 52
- count_chars() syntax: 53
- create database syntax: 53
- create database syntax: 54
- create table syntax: 54
- create table syntax: 55
- crypt() syntax: 55
- ctype_alnum() syntax: 56
- ctype_alpha() syntax: 56
- current() syntax: 56
- date() syntax: 57
- dechex() syntax: 57
- define() syntax: 57
- delete record syntax: 58
- delete record syntax: 58
- describe table syntax: 58
- die() syntax: 59
- do-while loop syntax: 59
- drop a field syntax: 59
- each() syntax: 60
- echo syntax: 60
- error_log() syntax: 60
- empty() syntax: 61
- encapsulation syntax: 61
- enctype syntax: 62
- end() syntax: 62
- explain table syntax: 62
- exit() syntax: 63
- explode() syntax: 63
- extends syntax: 63
- eval() syntax: 64

exec() syntax: 64
extract() syntax: 65
fclose() syntax: 65
feof() syntax: 65
fgetc() syntax: 66
fgetcvs() syntax: 66
fgets() syntax: 66
file() syntax: 66
fileatime() syntax: 66
filemtime() syntax: 67
file uploading syntax: 67
file_exists() syntax: 68
filesize() syntax: 68
file_get_contents() syntax: 68
file_put_contents() syntax: 68
filter_callback syntax: 69
filter_has_var() syntax: 69
filter_input syntax: 69
filter_input_array() syntax: 70
filter_var() syntax: 70
filter_var_array() syntax: 71
final syntax: 71
floatval() syntax: 71
floor() syntax: 72
flush() syntax: 72
fopen() syntax: 72
for loop syntax: 73
foreach() syntax: 73
fprintf() syntax: 73
fputs() syntax: 74
fread() syntax: 74
fscanf() syntax: 74
ftruncate() syntax; 75
function syntax: 75

- function with argument syntax: 75
- fwrite() syntax: 76
- getcwd() syntax: 76
- getdate() syntax: 76
- get_resource_type() syntax: 77
- getenv() syntax: 77
- getFile() syntax: 77
- getLine() syntax: 77
- getMessage() syntax: 78
- global variable syntax: 78
- gmdate() syntax: 79
- gmmktime() syntax: 79
- header syntax; 79
- heredoc syntax: 79
- htmlentities() syntax: 80
- html_entity_decode() syntax: 80
- htmlspecialchars() syntax: 80
- htmlspecialchars_decode() syntax: 81
- http_build_query() syntax: 81
- iconv() syntax: 81
- if statement syntax: 82
- if-else Statement syntax: 82
- if…elseif…else syntax: 82
- implode() syntax: 83
- in_array() syntax: 83
- include() syntax: 83
- include_once() syntax: 84
- insert into table syntax: 84
- insert into table syntax: 85
- insert into table syntax: 86
- intdiv() syntax: 86
- interface syntax: 86
- is_dir() syntax: 87
- is_file() syntax: 87

- is_int() syntax: 87
- is_integer() syntax: 88
- is_null() syntax: 88
- is_numeric() syntax: 88
- is_readable() syntax: 88
- is_string() syntax: 88
- isset() syntax: 89
- is_executable() syntax: 89
- is_writable() syntax: 89
- is_writeable() syntax: 89
- json_decode() syntax: 90
- json_encode() syntax: 90
- key() syntax: 90
- krsort() syntax: 90
- ksort() syntax: 91
- less / more than syntax: 91
- limit records syntax: 91
- list() syntax: 92
- local variable syntax: 92
- log() syntax: 92
- ltrim() syntax: 93
- mail() syntax: 93
- max() syntax: 93
- md5() syntax: 93
- md5_file() syntax: 94
- microtime() syntax: 94
- min() syntax: 94
- mkdir() syntax: 94
- mktime() syntax: 95
- move_uploaded_file() syntax: 95
- mt_rand() syntax: 95
- mysqli_affected_rows() syntax: 95
- mysqli_close( ) syntax: 96
- mysqli_connect() syntax: 96

- mysqli_connect_error() syntax: 96
- mysqli_data_seek() syntax: 97
- mysqli_error() syntax: 97
- mysqli_fetch_array() syntax: 97
- mysqli_fetch_assoc() syntax: 98
- mysqli_fetch_row() syntax: 99
- mysqli_free_result() syntax: 100
- mysqli_get_server_info() syntax: 100
- mysqli_num_rows() syntax: 101
- mysqli_query() syntax: 101
- mysqli_real_escape_string() syntax: 101
- mysqli_result() syntax: 101
- mysqli_select_db() syntax: 102
- namespace syntax: 102
- natcasesort() syntax: 103
- natsort() syntax: 103
- next() syntax: 103
- nl2br() syntax: 104
- not equal syntax: 104
- null value syntax: 105
- number_format() syntax: 105
- ob_clean() syntax: 105
- ob_end_clean() syntax: 105
- ob_end_flush() syntax: 106
- ob_flush() syntax: 106
- ob_get_clean() syntax: 106
- ob_get_flush() syntax: 106
- ob_get_contents() syntax: 107
- ob_get_length() 107
- ob_get_level() syntax: 108
- ob_start() syntax: 108
- object syntax: 108
- order by syntax: 109
- overloading syntax: 109

- override syntax: 109
- parent::__construct() syntax: 110
- parse_str() syntax: 111
- PHP_EOL syntax: 111
- phpinfo() syntax: 111
- pi() syntax: 111
- polymorphism syntax: 112
- pow() syntax: 112
- preg_match() syntax: 113
- preg_match_all() syntax: 113
- preg_replace() syntax: 113
- preg_split() syntax: 114
- prepare() syntax: 114
- prev() syntax: 114
- print syntax: 115
- printf() syntax: 115
- print_r() syntax: 115
- private syntax: 116
- protected syntax: 116
- public syntax: 117
- putenv() syntax: 118
- query() syntax: 118
- radio button syntax: 118
- rand() syntax: 119
- readfile() syntax: 119
- remove database syntax: 120
- remove table syntax: 120
- rename() syntax: 120
- require() syntax: 120
- require_once() syntax: 121
- reset form syntax: 121
- reset() syntax: 122
- return syntax: 122
- rmdir() syntax: 122

- round() syntax: 122
- rsort() syntax: 122
- rtrim() syntax: 123
- scandir() syntax: 123
- select data syntax: 123
- select data syntax: 124
- select to show table syntax: 125
- select option syntax: 125
- serialize() syntax: 126
- session_destroy() syntax: 126
- session_id()syntax: 127
- session_name() syntax: 128
- session_regenerate_id() syntax: 128
- session_start() syntax: 128
- session_status() syntax: 129
- session_unset() syntax: 129
- session_write_close() syntax: 130
- set_error_handler() syntax: 130
- set_exception_handler() syntax: 131
- setcookie() syntax: 131
- sha1() syntax: 132
- sha1_file() syntax: 132
- show databases syntax: 132
- show specified field syntax: 132
- show specified record syntax: 133
- show tables syntax: 134
- shuffle() syntax: 134
- simplexml_load_file() syntax: 135
- simplexml_load_string() syntax: 135
- sleep() syntax: 136
- sort() syntax: 136
- sort table data syntax: 136
- sprintf() syntax: 137
- sqrt() syntax: 137

- sscanf() syntax: 138
- static syntax: 138
- static member syntax: 138
- string syntax: 139
- string connecting syntax: 139
- stripos() syntax: 140
- stripslashes() syntax: 140
- stristr() syntax: 140
- strip_tags() syntax: 140
- str_ireplace() syntax: 140
- strlen( ) syntax: 141
- str_pad() syntax: 141
- strpbrk() syntax: 141
- strpos() syntax: 141
- str_repeat() syntax: 142
- strrev() syntax: 142
- strripos() syntax: 142
- strrpos() syntax: 142
- strstr() syntax: 142
- strtolower( ) syntax: 143
- strtotime() syntax: 143
- strtoupper() syntax: 143
- str_replace() syntax: 143
- str_shuffle() syntax: 144
- str_split() syntax: 144
- str_word_count() syntax: 144
- strtr() syntax: 144
- submit form syntax: 145
- substr() syntax: 145
- substr_count() syntax: 145
- substr_replace() syntax: 145
- switch syntax: 146
- text input syntax: 146
- textarea input syntax: 147

time() syntax: 147

trait syntax: 148

trigger_error() syntax: 148

trim() syntax: 148

try / throw / catch() syntax: 149

ucfirst() syntax: 149

ucwords() syntax: 149

uniqid() syntax: 150

unlink() syntax: 150

unserialize() syntax: 150

unset() syntax: 150

update table syntax: 151

update table syntax: 152

urldecode() syntax: 152

urlencode() syntax: 153

Use Database syntax: 153

usleep() syntax: 153

variable syntax: 153

var_dump() syntax: 154

where condition syntax: 154

while Loop syntax: 154

wordwrap() syntax: 154

xml dom parser syntax: 155

Appendix 156

PHP Reserved Words Chart 156

PHP Escaping Characters Chart 156

PHP Predefined Characters Chart 156

PHP File Opening Mode Chart 157

PHP Email Functions Chart 157

PHP Filter Functions Chart..157

PHP File Permission Chart 158

PHP String Format Chart 158

PHP Data & Time Format Chart..159

PHP Data Type Chart 159
mysqli_xxx_xxx ( ) Chart 160
MySQL Database Commands Chart 161
MySQL Table Commands Chart 161
MySQL Operation Commands Chart 161
MySQL Data Type Chart 162
MySQL Field Modifier Chart 162
MySQL System Function Chart 162
MySQL Numeric Function Chart 163
MySQL Datetime Function Chart 163
MySQL Statement Chart 164
Cheat Sheet by Ray Yao 168

Syntax Chart

<!-- --> syntax:

<!-- html comment -->

// The <!-- --> is a comment symbol of html

// PHP or HTML compiler always ignores the html comment.

e.g.

<html>

Hello World! <!-- show Hello World! -->

</html>

// Output: Hello World!

__call() syntax:

function __call($funName, $arg){...}

// __call() is invoked when an inexistent function is called in an object context.

// $funName is the function name, $arg is an array parameter.

e.g.

<?php

class MyClass{

public function **__call($funName, $arg)**{

echo "Calling '$funName' ". implode(' ', $arg);

}}

$obj = new MyClass;

$obj -> **myFun**('that is inexistent');   // myFun isn't existing in fact

?>

// Output: Calling 'myFun' that is inexistent

__callstatic() syntax:

function __callstatic($funName, $arg){...}

// __callstatic() is invoked when an inexistent function is called in a static context.

// $funName is the function name, $arg is an array parameter

e.g.

```php
<?php
class MyClass{
public static function __callStatic($funName, $arg){
echo "Calling '$funName' ". implode(' ', $arg);
}}
$obj = new MyClass;
MyClass::myFun( 'that is inexistent' );   // myFun isn't existing in fact
?>
// Output:   Calling 'myFun' that is inexistent
```

__construct() syntax:

function __construct($arg);

// Constructor is used to initialize the class's variables

e.g.

```php
<?php
class Flower{    // define a class "Flower"
var $c;
function __construct($arg) {   // constructor
$this->c= $arg;    // initialize the variable "c"
}}   // $this represents the current object $obj
$obj= new Flower( 'beautiful' );     // create an object "$obj"
echo $obj->c;
?>
// Output:  beautiful
```

__destruct() syntax:

function __destruct{}

// Destructor release the constructor resources. The destructor will be called when the object is destroyed or the program is stopped or exited.

e.g.

```php
<?php
```

```
class Flower{
var $c;
function __construct($arg) {    // define a constructor
$this->c= $arg;   echo $this->c;
}
function __destruct( ) {   // define a destructor
echo " Destructor runs… ";
}}
$obj= new Flower( ' Constructor runs… ' );
?>
// Output:    Constructor runs…  Destructor runs…
```

$_COOKIE[ ] syntax:

setcookie ("name", "value");   // set cookie name and value
$_COOKIE["name"]; // get cookie value by cookie name
e.g.

```
<!-- aFile.php -->
<?php  // in aFile.php
setcookie("color", "blue");   // set a cookie
// cookie name is "color", cookie value is "blue"
header("location: bFile.php");      // redirect to bFile.php
?>
```
<!--save this file with the name "aFile.php" in the working folder-->

```
<!-- bFile.php -->
<?php  // in bFile.php
$mycolor = $_COOKIE["color"];  // get the cookie from aFile.php
// get the cookie whose name is "color"
echo $mycolor;    // show the color's value
?>
```
<!--save the file with the name "bFile.php" in the working folder-->
<!--please run the aFile.php-->
// Output: blue

$_ENV syntax:

$_ENV["VARIABLE"]

// Contain the information about the environment variables.

e.g.

$_ENV["USER"] = "Ray Yao";

echo 'The username is: ' .$_ENV["USER"];

// Output:

The username: Ray Yao

$_FILE syntax:

$_FILES['file']['name'] // The name of the file to be uploaded.

$_FILES['file']['type'] // The mime type of the file.

$_FILES['file']['size'] // The byte size of the uploaded file.

$_FILES['file']['tmp_name'] // The temporary file name in server.

$_FILES['file']['error'] // The error information of the uploaded file.

e.g. // Assume that we upload a file named "myFile.txt"

```
<form action="" method="post" enctype="multipart/form-data">
<input type="file" name="file">
<input type ="submit" value="Submit">
</form>
<?php
echo "File Name: " . $_FILES['file']['name']."<br>";
echo "File Type : " . $_FILES['file']['type']."<br>";
echo "File Size : " . $_FILES['file']['size']."<br>";
echo "Temp Name: " . $_FILES['file']['tmp_name']."<br>";
echo "Error Info: " . $_FILES['file']['error']. "<br>";
?>
```

// Output:

[Choose File] myFile.txt   [Submit]

File Name: myFile.txt

File Type : text/plain

File Size : 279

Temp Name: C:\Windows\Temp\php5167.tmp

Error Info: 0

$_GET[ ] syntax:

$myData=$_GET[data];

// Get data from the HTML form and assigns its value to $myData.

e.g.

<html>

<form action=" " method="get">

<input type="text" name="data">

<!-- the inputted value will be stored to the "data" -->

<!--"data" will be passed to the PHP file for processing. -->

</form>

<?php   // Assume that we input "Hello, World!" in the text box

$myData = $_GET[data];

// $_GET[data] gets the "data" value from the html form

echo ("You have inputted: ".$myData);   // show data value

?>

</html>

// Output

| Hello, World! |

You have inputted: Hello, World!

$_POST[ ] syntax:

$myData=$_POST[data];

// Post data from the HTML form and assigns its value to $myData.

e.g.

<html>

<form action=" " method="post">

<input type="text" name="data">

<!-- the inputted value will be stored to the "data" -->

<!--"data" will be passed to the PHP file for processing. -->

</form>

```php
<?php   // Assume that we input "Hello, World!" in the text box
$myData = $_POST[ data ];
// $_POST[ data ] posts the "data" value from the html form
echo ("You have inputted: ".$myData);    // show data value
?>
</html>
```
// Output

| Hello, World! |

You have inputted: Hello, World!

$_REQUEST[ ] syntax:

$myData=$_REQUEST[data];

// Obtain data from the HTML form and assigns its value to $myData.

e.g.

```html
<html>
<form action=" "  method="request">
<input type="text"  name="data">
<!-- the inputted value will be stored to the "data" -->
<!--"data" will be passed to the PHP file for processing. -->
</form>
<?php   // Assume that we input "Hello, World!" in the text box
$myData = $_REQUEST[data];
// $_REQUEST[data] gets the "data" value from the html form
echo ("You have inputted: ".$myData);    // show data value
?>
</html>
```
// Output

| Hello, World! |

You have inputted: Hello, World!

$_SERVER[ ] syntax:

$_SERVER["HTTP_USER_AGENT"];

// Return the information about the browser of a visitor

e.g.

$browser = **$_SERVER["HTTP_USER_AGENT"]**;

echo "$browser";

// Output: Mozilla/4.0 (compatible; MSIE 8.0)…

$_SERVER["REQUEST_METHOD"] syntax:

$_SERVER["REQUEST_METHOD"]

// Returns the request method used to access the page

e.g.

```
<?php
$name = "";
if ($_SERVER["REQUEST_METHOD"]=="POST"){
// check if the form can be submitted
$name = $_POST["name"];
}
?>
<form method="post" action="">
Name: <input type="text" name="name">
</form>
<?php echo $name; ?>
```

// Output:

Name: | Ray Yao |

Ray Yao

$_SESSION[ ] syntax:

$_SESSION["name"] = value;   // set session name & value

$_SESSION["name"];   // get session value by name

e.g.

1.   <!-- aFile.php -->

<?php session_start( );

$_SESSION ["color"] = "green";   // set color as green

header("location: bFile.php");

?>   <!-- save this file as aFile.php -->

2. <!-- bFile.php -->
```
<?php  session_start( );
$carColor = $_SESSION ["color"];   // get the value of color
echo $carColor;
?>       <!-- save this file as bFile.php -->
```
<!-- please run the aFile.php -->
// Output: green

$_SERVER['PHP_SELF'] syntax:
action="<?php echo($_SERVER['PHP_SELF']);?>"
// Send form data to the current page instead of another page.
e.g.
```
<html>
<form action="<?php echo($_SERVER['PHP_SELF']);?>" method="post">
Name: <input type="text" name="myName">
<input type="submit" value="Submit">
</form>
<?php echo $_POST["myName"]; ?><br>
</html>
```
// Output:

Name: | Ray Yao | [Submit]

Ray Yao

$GLOBALS syntax:
$GLOBALS['variable']
// $GLOBALS is a PHP super global variable that is accessible in all scopes of a PHP program
e.g.
```
<?php
$a = 100; $b = 200;
function fun() {
$GLOBALS['c'] = $GLOBALS['a'] + $GLOBALS['b'];
```

}
fun();
echo $c;
?>
// Output: 300

$PHP_SELF syntax:

action="<?php echo($PHP_SELF);?>"

// Send form data to the current page instead of another page.

e.g.

<html>

<form **action="<?php echo($PHP_SELF);?>"** method="post">

Name: <input type="text" name="myName">

<input type="submit" value="Submit">

</form>

<?php echo $_POST["myName"]; ?>

</html>

// Output:

Name: Ray Yao   Submit

Ray Yao

$this syntax:

$this -> property;

//"$this -> property;" is used to access the property in the current class.

// $this represents the current object.

// Note: the property has no $ symbol in the "$this -> property"

e.g.

<?php

class ThisDemo{   // define a class "ThisDemo"

var $t = "\$this syntax example";

function myFun() {

echo **$this->t**;   // $this represents $obj

}}

```
$obj= new ThisDemo();    // create an object
$obj->myFun();   // $obj references the myFun(){ }
?>
```
// Output: $this syntax example

=> syntax:

array(key1=>value1, key2=>value2, kay3=>value3…);

// "=>" symbol is used to connect key and value.

// key and index is the same meaning in Array.

e.g.

```
<?php
$book=array( "A"=>"JSP", "B"=>"ASP", "C"=>"PHP");
```
// "A, B, C" are keys, "JSP, ASP, PHP" are values.

`echo $book[ "C" ];`   // show the element value in the key "C"

```
?>
```
// Output: PHP

== syntax:

value1 == value2

// Compare two values, but not compare the type of two values

e.g.

`if(`**`9 == "9"`**`){ echo 'equal'; }`

`else{ echo 'not equal'; }`

// Output: equal

=== syntax:

value1 === value2

// Compare two values, and compare the type of two values

e.g.

`if(`**`9 === "9"`**`){echo 'equal';}`

`else{ echo 'not equal';}`

// Output: not equal

++$var and $var++ syntax:

++$var   // $var plus 1, and return $var

$var++   // returns $var, and then $var plus 1

e.g.

$x=100; echo **++$x;**   // Output 101

$y=100; echo **$y++;**   // Output 100

--$var and $var-- syntax:

--$var   // $var minus 1, and return $var

$var--   // returns $var, and then $var minus 1

e.g.

$x=100; echo **--$x;**   // Output 99

$y=100; echo **$y--;**   // Output 100

? : operator syntax:

(test-expression) ? (if-true-do-this) : (if-false-do-this);

// Conditional operator checks if the test-expression is true or false, then, according to true or false to execute the specified block.

e.g.

$a = 100; $b = 200;

$result = ($a<$b) ? "apple " : "banana ";

// (check if $a<$b) ? (if-true-do-this) : (if-false-do-this);

echo ("$result
");

// Output: apple

<=> syntax:

$c = $a <=> $b;

// If $a > $b, then the value of $c is 1.

// If $a == $b, the value of $c is 0.

// If $a < $b, then the value of $c is -1.

e.g.

echo 10 **<=>** 10;   // 0

echo 3.14 **<=>** 3.10;   // 1

echo "ant" **<=>** "bee";   // -1

__class__ syntax:

__class__

// Return the current class name.

e.g.

```
<?php
class MyClass {
function myFun() {
echo 'The current class name is ' . __class__ ;
}}
$obj = new MyClass();
$obj->myFun();
?>
```

// Output: The current class name is MyClass

__dir__ syntax:

__dir__

// Return the directory of the current file

e.g.

echo 'The directory of the current file is ' . __dir__ ;

// Output: The directory of the current file is C:\AppServ\www

---

__file__ syntax:

__file__

// Return the current file path and file name

e.g.

echo 'The current file path and file name are ' . __file__ ;

// Output:

The current file path and file name are C:\AppServ\www\myFile.php

---

__function__ syntax:

__function__

// Return the current function name.

e.g.

```
<?php
```

```
function myFun() {
echo 'The current function name is ' . __function__ ;
}
myFun();
?>
// Output:   The current function name is myFun
```

__line__ syntax:

__line__

// Return the current line number in the file

e.g.

echo ' The current line number is ' . __line__ ;

// Output: The current line number is 2.

__method__ syntax:

__method__

// Return the method name of a class

e.g.

```
function myFun() {
echo 'The function name is ' . __method__ ;
}
myFun();
```

// Output: The function name is myFun

__namespace__ syntax:

__namespace__

// Return the name of namespace.

e.g.

namespace MyNamespace;

echo 'The namespace is ', __namespace__;

// Output: The namespace is MyNamespace.

__trait__ syntax:

__trait__

// Return a trait name.
// Trait is used to define a method that can be used in multiple classes.
// Trait enables programmers to reuse a method in different classes.
e.g.

```php
<?php
trait myTrait{
function myFun(){
echo 'The trait name is ' . __trait__ ;  // return the trait name
}}
class MyClass{
use myTrait;
}
$obj = new MyClass;
$obj->myFun();
?>
```

// Output: The trait name is myTrait

----

abs() syntax:

abs(number)

// Return the absolute value of different numbers
e.g.
echo(**abs**(-12.345));
// Output: 12.345

----

abstract syntax:

abstract BaseClass{abstract method();}
class DerivedClass implements BaseClass{method(){}}

// Abstracts class and method are defined by the abstract keyword.
// An abstract class contains at least one abstract method. Abstract method has no body, but need its derived class to complete the task.
// The method of the derived class can override the abstract method of the abstract base class.
e.g.
```php
<?php
```

```php
abstract class Base {    // define a abstract class
    abstract function show();    // define a abstract method
}
class Derived extends Base {
    function show() {
        echo "Implement the abstract function";
    }
}
$obj = new Derived;
$obj->show();
?>
```
// Output: Implement the abstract function

---

addslashes() syntax:

addslashes(" single quote or double quote ")

// Add a backslash in front of each single quote double quote.

e.g.

$str = **addslashes**("This is a 'good' food!");

echo($str);

// Output: This is a \'good\' food!

---

alter table syntax:

$sql="alter table tableName add columnName data type";
$query=mysqli_query($con, $sql);

// $sql="alter table tableName add columnName data type" is used to add a new column in the table.

// $query=mysqli_query($con, $sql) executes the query.

// "$con" is the connection to MySql server. (See mysqli_connect()).

e.g.

```php
<?php
$con= mysqli_connect( "localhost", "root", "12345678" );
if( $con ) {    // if connect MySQL server successfully
    echo " Connect successfully! ";
}
$select=mysqli_select_db( $con, "myDB" );
```

```
if( $select ) {    // if select database "myDB" successfully
echo  " Select myDB successfully!<br> ";
}    // assume that myDB has a table "colortable"
$sql="alter table colortable add column color5 varchar(20)";
// add a column "color5" into the table, type is "varchar(20)"
$query=mysqli_query( $con, $sql);    // execute query
if( $query ) {
echo  " Add a column successfully! ";
}
?>
```
// Output:

Connect successfully! Select myDB successfully!

Add a column successfully!

---

alter table syntax:

alter table TableName add FieldName type modifier;   // add a field

alter table TableName add primary key (FieldName);   // add a primary key

alter table TableName add unique (FieldName);   // add an unique property

alter table TableName alter FieldName set/drop default;   // alter default value

alter table TableName change FieldName1 FieldName2...;   // change fieldname

alter table TableName drop FieldName;   // remove a field

alter table TableName drop primary key;   // remove a primary key

alter table TableName modify FieldName type modifier;   // modify type/modifier

e.g.

use library;

alter table books

add pages int not null,

change author writer char(20);

explain books;

```
+--------+--------------+------+-----+---------+----------------+
| Field  | Type         | Null | Key | Default | Extra          |
+--------+--------------+------+-----+---------+----------------+
| id     | int(11)      | NO   | PRI | NULL    | auto_increment |
| title  | varchar(30)  | NO   |     | NULL    |                |
| price  | decimal(6,2) | NO   |     | NULL    |                |
| writer | char(20)     | YES  |     | NULL    |                |
| pages  | int(11)      | NO   |     | NULL    |                |
+--------+--------------+------+-----+---------+----------------+
```

// "add pages int not null," adds a new field "pages".

// "change author writer char(20);" changes the old field name "author" to a new field name "writer".

// After explaining the table, we can see:

// A new field "pages" has been added.

// The old field name "author" has been changed to new field name "writer".

---

arithmetical operator syntax:

$variable1 operator $variable2

// Assignment operators are "+, -, *, /, %, -"

// "%" gets remainder, "-" changes sign or subtracts a value

e.g.

$x=10; $y=2;

echo ($x + $y);   // output: 12

echo PHP_EOL;

echo ($x - $y);   // output: 8

echo PHP_EOL;

echo ($x * $y);   // output: 20

echo PHP_EOL;

echo ($x / $y);   // output: 5

echo PHP_EOL;

echo ($x % $y);   // output: 0

echo PHP_EOL;

echo -$x;   // output: -10

---

array_change_key_case() syntax:

array_change_key_case($array, CASE_UPPER / CASE_LOWER)

// Convert all keys in an array to lowercase or uppercase

e.g.

$score=array("Alf"=>"85","Bob"=>"92","Cin"=>"90");

print_r(**array_change_key_case**($score,CASE_UPPER));

// Output: Array([ALF] => 85   [BOB] => 92   [CIN] => 90)

---

array_chunk() syntax:

array_chunk ($array, size)

// Split an array into multiple arrays of a specific size

e.g.

$letter=array ("A", "B", "C", "D", "E", "F");

print_r(**array_chunk($letter,3)**);   // each array with 3 elements

// Output:

Array(

   [0] => Array([0] => A   [1] => B   [2] => C)

   [1] => Array([0] => D   [1] => E   [2] => F)

)

---

array_combine() syntax:

array_combine($arr1,$arr2);

// Combine two arrays, arr1 becomes keys, arr2 becomes values

e.g.

$arr1 = array("0","1","2");

$arr2 = array("a","b","c");

$cb = **array_combine($arr1,$arr2);**

print_r($cb);

// Output: Array([0] => a   [1] => b   [2] => c)

---

array_count_values() syntax:

array_count_values($arr)

// Return an array using the values as keys, the frequency as values.

e.g.

$arr=array("A","B","C","A","C","C");   // 2A, 1B, 3C

print_r(**array_count_values($arr)**);

// Output: Array ([A] => 2   [B] => 1   [C] => 3)

---

array creating syntax:

$arrayName = array ("value0", "value1", "value2",…);

// Create an array with multiple elements

// The index of array starts with zero

e.g.

$arr = array ("A", "B", "C");   // create an array $arr

echo $arr[0]; echo $arr[1]; echo $arr[2];

// Output: A B C

---

array creating syntax:

$arrayName = array ( );

$arrayName[index0] = "value0";

$arrayName[index1] = "value1";

$arrayName[index2] = "value2";

// Create an array with multiple elements

// The index of array starts with zero

e.g.

$color = array( );   // create an array $color

$color[0]='red '; $color[1]='yellow '; $color[2]='green ';

echo "$color[0]"; echo "$color[1]";echo "$color[2]";

// Output: red yellow green

---

array_diff() syntax:

array_diff($array1,$array2);

// Compare the values of two arrays, return the differences

e.g.

$a1=array("0"=>"a","1"=>"b","2"=>"c","3"=>"d");

$a2=array("4"=>"a","5"=>"b","6"=>"c");

$diff=**array_diff($a1,$a2);**

print_r($diff);

// Output: Array([3] => d)

---

array_diff_assoc() syntax:

array_diff_assoc($array1,$array2);

// Compare keys and values of two arrays, return the differences

e.g.

$a1=array("0"=>"a","1"=>"b","2"=>"c","3"=>"d");

$a2=array("0"=>"a","1"=>"b","2"=>"c");

$diff=**array_diff_assoc($a1,$a2)**;

print_r($diff);

// Output: Array([3] => d)

---

array_diff_key() syntax:

array_diff_key($array1,$array2);

// Compare the keys of two arrays, return the differences

e.g.

$a1=array("0"=>"a","1"=>"b","2"=>"c","3"=>"d");

$a2=array("0"=>"a","1"=>"b","2"=>"c");

$diff=**array_diff_key($a1,$a2)**;

print_r($diff);

// Output: Array([3] => d)

---

array_fill() syntax:

array_fill(start, number, value)

// Fill an array with the same values.

// "start": the start index, "number": the number of elements.

e.g.

$arr=**array_fill(2,3,"ok")**;

print_r($arr);

Output: Array([2] => ok   [3] => ok   [4] => ok)

---

array_fill_keys() syntax:

array_fill_keys($keys,"values")

// Fill an array with specified keys and the same values.

e.g.

$keys=array("1","2","3");   // set different keys

$arr=**array_fill_keys($keys,"ok")**;

print_r($arr);

// Output: Array([1] => ok   [2] => ok   [3] => ok)

---

array_flip() syntax:

array_flip($array)

// Flip all keys and their related values in an array

e.g.

$arr=array("1"=>"a","2"=>"b","3"=>"c");

$result=**array_flip($arr);**

print_r($result);

// Output: Array([a] => 1   [b] => 2   [c] => 3)

---

array_intersect() syntax:

array_intersect($array1,$array2);

// Compare all values of two arrays, return an array with the same values.

e.g.

$arr1=array("0"=>"a","1"=>"b","2"=>"c","3"=>"d");

$arr2=array("4"=>"a","5"=>"b","6"=>"c");

$result=**array_intersect($arr1,$arr2);**

print_r($result);

// Output: Array([0] => a   [1] => b   [2] => c)

---

array_intersect_assoc() syntax:

array_intersect_assoc($array1,$array2);

// Compare all keys and all values of two arrays, return an array with the same keys and the same values.

e.g.

$arr1=array("0"=>"a","1"=>"b","2"=>"c","3"=>"d");

$arr2=array("0"=>"a","1"=>"b","2"=>"c");

$result=**array_intersect_assoc($arr1,$arr2);**

print_r($result);

// Output: Array([0] => a   [1] => b   [2] => c)

---

array_intersect_key() syntax:

array_intersect_key($array1,$array2);

// Compare all keys of two arrays, return an array with the same keys.

e.g.

$arr1=array("0"=>"a","1"=>"b","2"=>"c","3"=>"d");

$arr2=array("0"=>"e","1"=>"f","2"=>"g");

$result=**array_intersect_key($arr1,$arr2);**

print_r($result);

// Output: Array([0] => a   [1] => b   [2] => c)

---

array_keys() syntax:

array_keys($array)

// Return all keys of the array.

e.g.

$arr=array("Alf"=>"90","Bob"=>"85","Cin"=>"92");

print_r(**array_keys($arr)**);

// Output: Array([0] => Alf   [1] => Bob   [2] => Cin)

---

array_key_exists() syntax:

array_key_exists("key", $array)

// Return true if the specified key exists in the array

e.g.

$arr=array("Alf"=>"90","Bob"=>"85","Cin"=>"92");

if (**array_key_exists("Bob",$arr)**){

echo "Bob exists!";

}

// Output: Bob exists!

---

array_merge() syntax:

array_merge(array1, array2);

// Merge array1 and array2, and create a new array.

e.g.

$array1=array ("A", "B", "C");

$array2=array ("D", "E", "F");

$array=array_merge($array1, $array2);   // merge arrays
foreach($array as $value) { echo("$value ");}
// Output: A B C D E F

---

array_multisort($arr) syntax:

array_multisort($arr);
// Return a sorted array in ascending order
e.g.
$arr=array("Cin","Alf","Dan","Bob");
array_multisort($arr);
print_r($arr);
// Output: Array([0]=>Alf   [1]=>Bob   [2]=>Cin   [3]=>Dan)

---

array_pad() syntax:

array_pad($arrary,size,value)
// Return an array with specified size, the rest array elements will be filled with the parameter value.
e.g.
$arr=array("a","b");
print_r(**array_pad($arr,4,"c")**); // rest elements will be filled with "c"
// Output: Array([0] => a   [1] => b   [2] => c   [3] => c)

---

array_pop() syntax:

array_pop(array);
// Remove the last element of the array.
e.g.
$arr=array("A", "B", "C", "END");
array_pop($arr);   // remove the last element
echo ("$arr[0], $arr[1], $arr[2]");
// Output: A, B, C

---

array_product() syntax:

array_product($array)
// Calculate and return the product of all element values in the array.

e.g.

$arr=array(10,20);

echo(**array_product($arr)**);

// Output: 200

---

array_push() syntax:

array_push(array, value1, value2…);

// array_push(array, value1, value2) adds value1, value2 at the end of the array.

e.g.

$arr=array("A", "B", "C");

array_push($arr, "END");

// add "END" to the end of the array

echo ("$arr[0], $arr[1], $arr[2], $arr[3]");

// Output: A, B, C, END

---

array_rand() syntax:

array_rand($array,size)

// Return a new array containing random keys of the original array.

// Parameter size specifies the length of the new array.

e.g.

$arr=array("a"=>"ant","b"=>"bee","c"=>"cat","d"=>"dog");

print_r(**array_rand($arr,2)**);

// Output: Array([0] => b   [1] => d)

---

array_reverse() syntax:

array_reverse($array)

// Return a new array in reversed order

e.g.

$arr=array("1"=>"a","2"=>"b","3"=>"c");

print_r(**array_reverse($arr)**);

// Output: Array([0] => c   [1] => b   [2] => a)

---

array_search() syntax:

array_serch("value", $array)

// Search an array for a key according to the array value.

e.g.

$a=array("a"=>"ant", "b"=>"bee", "c"=>"cat", "d"=>"dog");

echo **array_search("cat",$a);**   // return a key

// Output: c

---

array_shift() syntax:

array_shift(array);

// Remove the first element of the array.

e.g.

$arr=array("START", "A", "B", "C");

array_shift($arr);   // remove the first element

echo ("$arr[0], $arr[1], $arr[2]");

// Output: A, B, C

---

array size syntax:

count($array);

sizeof($array);

// Two functions can get the size of an array

e.g.

$color = array("yellow", "purple", "orange");

$size1= **count**($color);   // get the size of the array

$size2 = **sizeof**($color);   // get the size of the array

echo ("$size1 ");   echo ("$size2 ");

// Output: 3   3

---

array_slice() syntax:

array_slice(array, start, length);

// Extract some elements from an array, at the start position by specifying length, and create a new array.

e.g.

$array=array("A","B","C","D","E","F");

$arr=**array_slice($array, 2, 3);**

// extract three elements from index 2
foreach($arr as $value){ echo "$value ";}
// Output: C D E

---

array_splice() syntax:
array_splice($array1, offset, length, $array2)
// Replace the array1 elements with array2 elements according to the parameter offset and length.
e.g.
$a1=array("a"=>"ant","b"=>"bee","c"=>"cat", "d"=>"dog");
$a2=array("a"=>"awl","b"=>"bat");
array_splice($a1, 0, 2, $a2);   // replace two elements
print_r($a1);
// Output: Array([0]=>awl [1]=>bat [c]=>cat [d]=>dog)

---

array_sum() syntax:
array_sum($array)
// Return the sum of all element values in an array.
e.g.
$arr=array(10, 20, 30);
echo **array_sum($arr)**;
// Output: 60

---

array_unique() syntax:
array_unique($arr)
// Remove all duplicate values from an array
e.g.
$arr=array(10, 20 , 20, 20, 30);
print_r(**array_unique($arr)**);
// Output: Array([0] => 10   [1] => 20   [4] => 30)

---

array_unshift() syntax:
array_unshift(array, value1, value2…);

// array_unshift(array, value1, value2) adds value1, value2 at the beginning of the array.

e.g.

$arr=array("A", "B", "C");

array_unshift($arr, "START");

// add "START" to the beginning of the array

echo ("$arr[0], $arr[1], $arr[2], $arr[3]");

// Output: START, A, B, C

---

array_values() syntax:

array_values($array)

// Return a new array containing all values of the original array.

e.g.

$arr=array("a"=>"ant", "b"=>"bee", "c"=>"cat", "d"=>"dog");

print_r(**array_values($arr)**);

// Output: Array([0] => ant   [1] => bee   [2] => cat   [3] => dog)

---

arsort() syntax:

arsort($array)

// Sorts an associative array values in descending order.

e.g.

$score=array("Rosy"=>"90","Andy"=>"100","Jony"=>"85");

arsort($score);   // sort values

print_r($score);

// Output: Array([Andy] => 100   [Rosy] => 90   [Jony] => 85)

---

asort() syntax:

asort($array)

// Sorts an associative array values in ascending order.

e.g.

$score=array("Rosy"=>"90","Andy"=>"100","Jony"=>"85");

asort($score);   // sort values

print_r($score);

// Output: Array([Jony] => 85   [Rosy] => 90   [Andy] => 100)

---

assignment syntax:

x += y is the same as **x = x + y**
x -= y is the same as **x = x - y**
x *= y is the same as **x = x * y**
x /= y is the same as **x = x / y**
x %= y is the same as **x = x % y**
x .= y is the same as **x = x . y**

e.g.

$a=10; $a += 1; echo $a;   // output 11
$b=20; $b -= 2; echo $b;   // output 18
$c=30; $c *= 3; echo $c;   // output 90
$d=40; $d /= 4; echo $d;   // output 10
$e=50; $e %= 5; echo $e;   // output 0
$f=60; $g=70; $f.=$g; echo $f;   // output 6070

---

between… and… syntax:

where FieldName between…and…

// Select records in a certain range in a table.

e.g.

1. Given the current status of the table "books" as follows:

use library;

select * from books;

```
+----+-------+---------+-------+-------+---------+
| id | title | writer  | pages | price | publish |
+----+-------+---------+-------+-------+---------+
|  1 | Java  | Ray Yao |   200 | 13.99 |    2018 |
|  2 | Ajax  | Ann Lee |   190 | 12.88 |    2019 |
|  3 | Html  | Jan Poe |   110 | 10.99 |    2014 |
|  4 | Ruby  | Ray Yao |   200 | 13.99 |    2017 |
|  5 | Rust  | R.Y.    |   128 | 12.99 |    2016 |
|  6 | Node  | R.Y.    |   128 | 12.99 |    2020 |
|  7 | Lamp  | Jan Poe |   120 | 11.67 |    2015 |
+----+-------+---------+-------+-------+---------+
```

2. Show filtered data by using between…and…

select * from books **where** id **between** 3 **and** 5;

```
+----+-------+---------+-------+-------+---------+
| id | title | writer  | pages | price | publish |
+----+-------+---------+-------+-------+---------+
|  3 | Html  | Jan Poe |  110  | 10.99 |  2014   |
|  4 | Ruby  | Ray Yao |  200  | 13.99 |  2017   |
|  5 | Rust  | R.Y.    |  128  | 12.99 |  2016   |
+----+-------+---------+-------+-------+---------+
```
// "where id between 3 and 5;" only selects the id from 3 and 5.

---

break statement syntax:

if (// condition **) break;**

// "break" keyword is used to stop the running of a loop according to the condition.

e.g.

```php
<?php
$num=0;
while ($num<10){
if ($num==5) break;   // exit the current loop if $num is 5
$num++;
}
echo ( $num );
?>
```
// Output: 5

---

ceil() syntax:

ceil(num)

// Return a closest integer that is greater than or equal to its argument.

e.g.

echo(**ceil(9.5)**);

// Output: 10

---

checkbox input syntax:

<input type="checkbox" name="data" value="myValue">

// type="checkbox" is used to input data by multiple choices.

// name="data" specifies the inputted data that will be passed to the PHP file for processing.

// value="myValue" specifies one of the optional contents.

e.g.

```php
<?php
$data = isset($_POST['data']) ? $_POST['data'] : "";
if(is_array($data)) {
   $books = array(
        'Matlab' => ' Matlab in 8 Hours. ',
        'Kotlin' => ' Kotlin in 8 Hours. ',
        'Pandas' => ' Pandas in 8 Hours. ',
   );
   foreach($data as $val) {
      echo $books[$val] . PHP_EOL;
   }
} else {
?><form action="" method="post">
   <input type="checkbox" name="data[]" value="Matlab">Matlab
   <input type="checkbox" name="data[]" value="Kotlin">Kotlin
   <input type="checkbox" name="data[]" value="Pandas">Pandas
   <input type="submit" value="Submit">
</form>
<?php
}
?>
```

// Output:

☐ Matlab ☑ Kotlin ☑ Pandas [Submit]

Kotlin in 8 Hours.   Pandas in 8 Hours.

----

chdir() syntax:

chdir("directory");

// Change the working directory to a specified directory

e.g.

echo getcwd() . "\n";   // get the current working directory

chdir('myDirectory');   // change to myDirectory

echo getcwd() . "\n";   // get the current working directory
// Output:
/home/study
/home/study/myDirectory

---

checkdate() syntax:
checkdate(mm, dd. yyyy)
// Check if a date is valid Gregorian date.
// The Gregorian date is the internationally accepted civil calendar.
e.g.
var_dump(**checkdate(10, 30, 2022)**);
var_dump(**checkdate(2, 30, 2021)**);
// Output: bool(true)   bool(false)

---

chmod() syntax:
chmod(file, mode)
// Change permissions of a file according to the parameter mode.
// The mode parameter has four numbers:
The 1st number is always zero
The 2nd number sets permissions for the owner
The 3rd number sets permissions for the group
The 4th number sets permissions for others
// The mode is set by adding up the following numbers:
1 = executing permissions
2 = writing permissions
4 = reading permissions
e.g.
chmod("myFile.txt",0720);   // Execute, write and read for owner, write for group, nothing for others
chmod("myFile.txt",0604);   // Write and read for owner, nothing for group, read for others.

---

chop() syntax:
chop($string, "substring")

// Remove a specified substring in the right end of a string.
e.g.
$str = "Java Cheat Sheet Book";
echo $str."\n";
echo **chop($str,"Book")**;
// Output: Java Cheat Sheet

---

chr() syntax:
chr(ascii)
// Return a character from the specified ASCII value
e.g.
echo **chr(56)** . " ";   // Decimal value
echo **chr(0x56)** . " ";   // Hex value
// Output: 8   V

---

chunk_split() syntax:
chunk_split($string, length, "separator")
// Split a string according to the specified length and separator.
e.g.
$str = "JavaScript";
echo **chunk_split($str,2,"-")**;
// Output: Ja-va-Sc-ri-pt-

---

class definition syntax:
class ClassName{   // define a class
var $variable;   // define a property
function function-name ( ){ }   // define a method
}
// A class is a template for an object, and creates an object.
// The class name is always capitalized
e.g.
class Car {   // define a class "Car"
var speed; var mileage;   // declare two property members
function run( ) {…}   // declare a method member

}

e.g.

```php
<?php
class MyClass{      // define a class
var $p = "A class & object example ";    // define a variable "$p"
}
$obj= new MyClass();    // create an object "obj"
echo $obj -> p;    // an object references a variable
?>
```
// Output: A class & object example

Class::method() syntax:

Class :: function( );

// A class can use :: to call a function directly.

e.g.

```php
<?php
class A {
function display( ) {
echo " Display() is called ";
}}
class B extends A {
function show() {
A :: display( );    // class A calls the function display(){ }
echo " Show() is called  ";
}}
B :: show( );    // class B calls the function show(){ }
?>
```
// Output: Display() is called   Show() is called

---

clearstatcache();

clearstatcache();

// Clear the cache of the file status

e.g.

```php
<?php    // assume that the original file size is 800 bytes.
echo filesize("myFile.txt");    // output file size 800 bytes.
$f = fopen("myFile.txt", "a+");
ftruncate($f,120);    // truncate the file to 120 bytes
fclose($f);
clearstatcache();    // clear cache
echo filesize("myFile.txt");    // check file size again
?>
// Output:   800   120
```

---

close connection syntax:

$conn->close();

// Close connection with MySQL.

e.g.

$conn = new mysqli("localhost","user","password","db");

$conn->close();

// The connection will be automatically closed after script finishes running. We can also use "mysqli_close($conn)" to close connection.

---

comment syntax:

// symbol is used in single-line comments.

/*......*/ symbols are used in multi-line comments.

e.g.

echo (" OK ");   // output OK.

echo (" Hello ");   /* echo ("Hello"); is a PHP output command, "echo" is a PHP reserved word, it shows or prints the word "Hello" in here. PHP is very easy to learn. */

// Output: OK   Hello

---

compact() syntax:

compact("val1", "val2", "val3",...);

// Create a new array by using some variables and values.

e.g.

$a="ant"; $b="bee"; $c="cat"; $d="dog";

```
$result = compact("a", "b", "c", "d");
print_r($result);
// Output:  Array( [a]=>ant   [b]=>bee   [c]=>cat   [d]=>dog )
```

---

conditional operator syntax:

(test-expression) ? (if-true-do-this) : (if-false-do-this);

// Conditional operator checks if the test-expression is true or false, then, according to true or false to execute the specified block.

e.g.

```
$a = 100; $b = 200;
$result = ($a<$b) ? "apple " : "banana ";
// (check if $a<$b) ? (if-true-do-this) : (if-false-do-this);
echo ("$result<br>");
// Output:   apple
```

---

connect MySQL syntax:

$con = new mysqli("servername", "username", "password");

// Connect MySQL

e.g.

```
<?php
$con = new mysqli("servername", "username", "password");
// Connect MySQL
if ($con->connect_error) {   // check connection
    die("Connection fails: " . $con->connect_error);
}
echo "Connection succeeds";
?>
// Output:   Connection succeeds
```

---

connect_error() syntax:

$conn -> connect_error

// An connection error happens, and return the error message of the connection with MySQL

e.g.

```php
<?php
$conn = new mysqli("localhost","user","password","db");
if ($conn -> connect_error) {
echo "Failed to connect to MySQL: " . $conn -> connect_error;
exit();
}
?>
```
// Output: Failed to connect to MySQL: No connection could be made because the target machine actively refused it.

---

const syntax:

const CONSTANT = value;

// The value of constant is immutable in runtime.

e.g.

const NAME = "Ray Yao";   // define a constant
echo NAME;

// Output: Ray Yao

---

constant() syntax:

constant("CONSTANT");

// Return the value of the CONSTANT.

e.g.

define("BOOK", "R in 8 Hours", true);
echo **constant("BOOK")**;

// Output: R in 8 Hours

---

constructor syntax:

function ClassName(){}

// Constructor is used to initialize the class's variables
// The constructor name is always the same as the class name

e.g.

```php
<?php
class Flower{    // define a class "Flower"
```

```
var $c;
function Flower( $arg ) {    // define a constructor
$this->c= $arg;    // initialize the variable "c"
}}
```
// $this represents the current object $obj

```
$obj= new Flower( 'beautiful' );    // create an object "$obj"
echo $obj->c;
?>
```
// Output: beautiful

---

continue statement syntax:

if (// condition **) continue;**

// "continue" is used to stop the current loop according to the condition, ignoring the subsequent code, and then continue the next loop.

e.g.
```
<?php
$num=0;
while ($num<10){
$num++;
if ($num==5) continue;    // go to the next loop if $num is 5
echo ( $num );    // skip echo($num) if $num is 5
}    // note:  the output has no the "5"
?>
```
// output: 1234678910

---

copy() syntax:

echo copy("source_file", "target_file");

// Copy the source file to the target file.

e.g.

echo copy("file1.txt","file2.txt");

// If the target file already exists, it will be overwritten.

---

count() syntax:

count($array)

// Count the numbers of elements in an array

e.g.

$arr=array("A","B","C");

echo **count($arr);**

// Output: 3

---

count_chars() syntax:

count_chars(string, mode)

// Return information about the string according to the following modes:

0 - an array with ASCII value as key, number of occurrences as value

1 - an array with ASCII value as key, number of occurrences as value (list number>0)

2 - an array with ASCII value as key, number of occurrences as value (list number=0)

3 - a string with all used characters.

4 - a string with all unused characters.

e.g.

$str = "Hello";

print_r(**count_chars($str,1)**);   // use mode 1

// Output: Array([72] => 1   [101] => 1   [108] => 2   [111] => 1)

// H is 72, e is 101, l is 108, o is 111.

---

create database syntax:

CREATE DATABASE dbName

// create a database

e.g.

<?php

$con = new mysqli("servername", "username", "password");   // connect

if ($con->connect_error) {   // check connection

die("Connection fails: " . $con->connect_error);

}

?>

$sql = "CREATE DATABASE myDatabase";   // create database

if ($con->query($sql) === TRUE) {

  echo "Create a database successfully";

```
} else {
  echo "Create a database unsuccessfully: " . $con->error;
}
$con->close();
?>
```
// Output: Create database successfully

---

create database syntax:
create database if not exists DatabaseName;

// Create a database in a mysql server

e.g.

create database if not exists garage;

show databases;

```
+--------------------+
| Database           |
+--------------------+
| garage             |
| garden             |
| information_schema |
| mysql              |
| performance_schema |
| sakila             |
| sys                |
| world              |
+--------------------+
```

// "create database if not exists garage;" creates a database named "garage" if this database does not exist currently.

---

create table syntax:
CREATE TABLE tableName

// Create a table

e.g.

```
<?php
```
$con=new mysqli("servername","username","password","db");

if ($con->connect_error) {   // check connection

die("Connection fails: " . $con->connect_error);

}

```
$sql = "CREATE TABLE myTable (   // create table
id INT(8) UNSIGNED AUTO_INCREMENT PRIMARY KEY,
firstname VARCHAR(28) NOT NULL,
lastname VARCHAR(28) NOT NULL,
)";
if ($con->query($sql) === TRUE) {
  echo "Create a table successfully";
} else {
  echo " Create a table unsuccessfully: " . $con->error;
}
$con->close();
?>
// Output:   Create a table successfully
```

---

create table syntax:

create table if not exists TableName (col1 type1, col2 type2, …);

// Create a table in the current database

e.g.

use world;

create table if not exists city_language(id int, name text);

show tables;

```
+-----------------+
| Tables_in_world |
+-----------------+
| city            |
| city_language   |
| country         |
| countrylanguage |
+-----------------+
```

// "use world;" selects a database "world" before handling with a table.

// "create table if not exists city_language;" creates a table named "city_language" if this table does not exist currently.

// "show tables" shows all existing tables in the current database.

---

crypt() syntax:

crypt($string);

// Execute a one-way encryption on the string using an algorism.

// Different platforms use different encryptions, such as Des, Md5…

e.g.

$password = "myPassword";

echo **crypt($password)**;   // output will vary

// Output: 1fZIP3vyr$gaHN3kr8.O/c9DgIo0GWZ.

---

ctype_alnum() syntax:

ctype_alnum($string);

// Return true if the string consists of alphanumeric characters.

// Non-alphanumeric characters are <?, <%, <!, #, $, %, ^, &, * , any other special symbols and spaces.

e.g.

$string = "JAVAin8hours";

if (**ctype_alnum($string)**){ echo "It's alphanumeric"; }

// Output: It's alphanumeric

---

ctype_alpha() syntax:

ctype_alpha($string);

// Return true if the string consists of alphabetic characters.

// Non-alphabetic characters are 0-9, <?, <%, <!, #, $, %, ^, &, * , any other special symbols and spaces.

e.g.

$string = "RayYao";

if (**ctype_alpha($string)**){ echo "It's alphabetic"; }

// Output: It's alphabetic

---

current() syntax:

current($array)

// Return the element which the current pointer points to, the first element by default.

e.g.

$arr = array("ant", "bee", "cat", "dog");

echo **current($arr)**;

// Output: ant

---

date() syntax:

date("M d Y");   // show month, date, year
date("h : i : s");   // show hour, minute, second
date("D H A");   // show day, hour, am/pm
date("d m Y");   // show day, month, year

1. e.g.

$date = **date("M d Y ");**
$hour = **date("h : i : s ");**
$week = **date("D H A ");**
echo $date; echo $hour; echo $week;
// Output: Nov 26 2015 02 : 29 : 02 Thu 14 PM

2. e.g.

```
<?php
echo date("Y/m/d") . " ";
echo date("Y.m.d") . " ";
echo date("Y-m-d") . " " ;
?>
```
// Output: 2022/11/08   2022.11.08   2022-11-08

---

dechex() syntax:

dechex(decimal_number)

// Convert a decimal number into a hexadecimal number.

e.g.

echo **dechex("60")." ";**
echo **dechex("80")." ";**
// Output: 3c   50

---

define() syntax:

define("NAME", "value", true);

// define a constant and value.
// "NAME": constant name. "value": constant value.
// "true": case insensitive. "false": case sensitive.

e.g.

define("BOOK", "R in 8 Hours", true);

echo BOOK;   echo " ";   echo book;

// Output: R in 8 Hours   R in 8 Hours

---

delete record syntax:

DELETE FROM tableName WHERE columnName = value

// Delete a record that meet the condition from a table

e.g.

$sql = "**DELETE FROM** myTable WHERE id=3";   // php code

// delete a recode where id is 3.

---

delete record syntax:

delete from tableName where fieldName = value;

// Remove a record in a table according to "where" statement.

e.g.

delete from myTable **where** id = 10;   // mysql code

// delete a record whose id is 10.

---

describe table syntax:

describe TableName;

// Show a table format, field name, data types and modifiers.

e.g.

use world;

describe city;

```
+-------------+----------+------+-----+---------+----------------+
| Field       | Type     | Null | Key | Default | Extra          |
+-------------+----------+------+-----+---------+----------------+
| ID          | int(11)  | NO   | PRI | NULL    | auto_increment |
| Name        | char(35) | NO   |     |         |                |
| CountryCode | char(3)  | NO   | MUL |         |                |
| District    | char(20) | NO   |     |         |                |
| Population  | int(11)  | NO   |     | 0       |                |
+-------------+----------+------+-----+---------+----------------+
```

// "describe city" can show the format of the table "city".

// Field: Column in the table. (e.g. ID is a column name.)

// Type: Data type of the column. (e.g. The data type of ID is int.)

// Null: Whether allow null or not. (e.g. ID doesn't allow null.)
// Key: Specify a primary key. (e.g. ID is set as a primary key.)
// Default: Specify a default value. (e.g. ID has no default value.)
// auto_increment: The field value increases automatically.

---

die() syntax:
die("message");
// Output a message and terminate the current program.
e.g.
fopen("myFile.txt","r")   // assume that myFile.txt doesn't exist
or **die("The file is no found!")**;
// Output: The file is no found!

---

do-while loop syntax:
do{ // some php codes in here **} while (test-expression);**
// Loops through a block of code once, and then repeats the loop if the specified condition is true.
e.g.
<?php
$counter=0;
do {
echo "@";
$counter++;   // increase 1 every loop
} while ($counter<8);   // loop at most 8 times
?>
// Output: @@@@@@@@

---

drop a field syntax:
alter table TableName drop FieldName;
// Remove a field of a table in a database.
e.g.
1. Given the current status of the table "books" as follows:
use library;
select * from books;

```
+----+-------+-------+---------+
| id | title | price | writer  |
+----+-------+-------+---------+
|  1 | Java  | 16.99 | Ray Yao |
|  2 | Ajax  | 12.88 | Ann Lee |
|  3 | Lamp  | 11.67 | Jan Poe |
+----+-------+-------+---------+
```

2. Remove a record and a field.

use library;

delete from books **where** id = 3;

alter table books **drop** price;

select * from books;

```
+----+-------+---------+
| id | title | writer  |
+----+-------+---------+
|  1 | Java  | Ray Yao |
|  2 | Ajax  | Ann Lee |
+----+-------+---------+
```

// "delete from books where id = 3;" removes a record whose id is 3.

// "alter table books drop price;" removes a field named "price".

----

each() syntax:

// This function has been deprecated since PHP 7.2.0.

----

echo syntax:

echo "content";

echo ("content");

// Output string or value of a variable.

e.g.

echo " Hello World! ";

echo (" Hello World! ");

// Output: Hello World!   Hello World!

// The different between "echo" and "print":

// "echo" can output one or more strings, without return value.

// "print" only outputs one string and can return a value 1.

----

error_log() syntax:

error_log(message, Error_num, destination, header)

// Save an error message to the specified destination on server

// Error number: 0 - send to server, 1 - send by email,
// 2 - send by php3, 3 - send and add to the existing file.
e.g.
error_log("An error happen!", 3, "/server/tmp/errorFile.log");
// The text will be saved in log.

---

empty() syntax:

empty($variable)
// Return true if the $variable is empty, return false if not.
e.g.
$var = 10;   // define a variable
if(**empty($var)**){echo "'var' is empty.";}
else{ echo "'var' is not empty";}
// Output: 'var' is not empty

---

encapsulation syntax:

class MyClass{
private $variable;   // define a private variable
function setVariable(){...}   // set the variable value
function getVariable(){...}   // get the variable value
}
// Encapsulation can hide the sensitive information from the user, ensure the security.
// Encapsulation wraps the similar properties and methods together in a single unit called class.
e.g.
```
<?php
class Income{    // encapsulation
  private $salary;    // define a private variable
  public function setSalary($arg){
    $this->salary = $arg;
  }
  public function getSalary(){
    return $this->salary;
```

```
    }
};
$m = new Income();
$m->setSalary(98000);
echo "Salary is $".$m->getSalary()." dollars per month";
?>
// Output:   Salary is $98000 dollars per month
```

---

enctype syntax:

‹form enctype="value">
// Specify which content type to use when submitting the form.

e.g.

<form **enctype** = "multipart/form-data">
// For unloading a file or submitting file data

<form **enctype** = "text/plain">
// Send data without any encoding

---

end() syntax:

end($array)
// Return the last element of an array.

e.g.

```
$arr = array("ant", "bee", "cat", "dog");
echo end($arr);
// Output:   dog
```

---

explain table syntax:

explain TableName;
// Show a table format, field name, data types and modifiers.

e.g.

use world;

explain city;

```
+-------------+----------+------+-----+---------+----------------+
| Field       | Type     | Null | Key | Default | Extra          |
+-------------+----------+------+-----+---------+----------------+
| ID          | int(11)  | NO   | PRI | NULL    | auto_increment |
| Name        | char(35) | NO   |     |         |                |
| CountryCode | char(3)  | NO   | MUL |         |                |
| District    | char(20) | NO   |     |         |                |
| Population  | int(11)  | NO   |     | 0       |                |
+-------------+----------+------+-----+---------+----------------+
```

// "explain city" can show the format of the table "city".

// Field: Column in the table. (e.g. ID is a column name.)

// Type: Data type of the column. (e.g. The data type of ID is int.)

// Null: Whether allow null or not. (e.g. ID doesn't allow null.)

// Key: Specify a primary key. (e.g. ID is set as a primary key.)

// Default: Specify a default value. (e.g. ID has no default value.)

// auto_increment: The field value increases automatically.

---

exit() syntax:

exit("message");

// Output a message and exit the current program.

e.g.

fopen("myFile.txt","r")   // assume that myFile.txt doesn't exist

or **exit("The file is no found!");**

// Output: The file is no found!

---

explode() syntax:

explode(separator,$str)

// Convert a string into an array

e.g.

$str = "R in 8 hours";

print_r (**explode(" ",$str)**);

// Output: Array([0]=>R   [1]=>in   [2]=>8   [3]=>hours)

---

extends syntax:

class sub-class extends parent-class {……}

// The child class can inherit all features of the parent class.

// The object of child class can reference the variable and function of the parent class.

e.g.

```php
<?php
class Animal{     // parent class
var $head;     // parent class's variable
function tail( ) {     // parent class's function
echo " Dog's tail is small ";
}}
class Dog extends Animal{ // child class inheritance parent class
}
$d = new Dog( );     // create an object of the child class
$d->head = "big"; // references the variable of the parent class
echo " Dog's head is ".$d->head." ";
$d->tail( );     // references the function of the parent class
?>
```
// Output: Dog's head is big   Dog's tail is small

---

eval() syntax:

eval($string)

// Evaluate a string as PHP code. The string must be valid PHP code and must end with semicolon.

e.g.

$str = '$num = 100; echo $num;';

eval($str);   // the $str is php code

// Output: 100

---

exec() syntax:

exec('external_program');

// Execute an external program or an external command.

e.g.

echo exec('whoami');

// The function will return the last line of the executed program's output.

---

extract() syntax:

extract($array);

// Convert array keys into variable names and array values into variable value.

e.g.

$arr=array("a"=>"ant", "b"=>"bee", "c"=>"cat", "d"=>"dog");

extract($arr);

echo "\$a=$a; \$b=$b; \$c=$c; \$d=$d";

// Output: $a=ant; $b=bee; $c=cat; $d=dog

---

fclose() syntax:

fcolse($openedFile);

// Close the opened file

// Release memory resource, other processes using the file

e.g.

$filename = "D:\myfile.txt";   // set the path D:\myfile.txt

$openfile = fopen($filename, w);   // open a file with w mode

$content = fwrite($openfile, "Hello!!");   // writing

fcolse($openfile);   // close the opened file

// After writing myfile.txt, we can use fclose() to close the opened file.

---

feof() syntax:

feof($file)

// Return true if reading reaches the end of file, return false if not.

e.g.

$f = fopen("myFile.txt","r");

while(**!feof($f)**){   // If don't read to the end of the file, keep running

  $contents = fgets($f);   // fgets($f) reads the file

  echo $contents. "<br>";

}

// Output: (The following text is the contents of the file)

Hi, this is myfile.txt, there are two lines in this file.

Here is the end of the file.

---

fgetc() syntax:

fgetc($file)

// Read one character from the specified file

e.g.

$f = fopen("myFile.txt","r");

echo **fgetc($f)**;

// Output: R

---

fgetcvs() syntax:

fgetcvs($file)

// Read one line from the cvs file

e.g.

$f = fopen("myFile.cvs","r");

print_r(**fgetcsv($f)**);

// Output: Array([0]=>ant   [1]=>bee   [2]=>cat   [3]=>dog)

---

fgets() syntax:

fgets($file)

// Read one line from the specified file

e.g.

$f = fopen("myFile.txt","r");

echo **fgets($f)**;

// Output: This is one line text in myFile.txt

---

file() syntax:

file("filename.txt")

// Read the contents of a file to an array

e.g.

print_r(**file("myFile.txt")**);

// Output: Array ([0]=>Hi, this is myFile.txt.   [1]=>There are two lines in this file.   [2]=>Here is the last line.)

---

fileatime() syntax:

fileatime("file.txt"))

// Return the last access time of the specified file

e.g.

echo "Last access: ".date("F d Y H:i:s.", **fileatime("myFile.txt")**);

// Output: Last access: May 17 2022 18:15:32.

----

filemtime() syntax:

filemtime("file.txt"))

// Return the last modifying time of the specified file

e.g.

echo "Last modified: ".date("F d Y H:i:s.", **filemtime("d:\myFile.txt")**);

// Output: Last access: May 17 2022 18:15:32.

----

file uploading syntax:

<input type="file" name="file">

// input type="file" specifies the form that is used to upload file.

// name="file" specifies the uploaded "file" that will be passed to the PHP file for processing.

e.g. // Assume that we upload a file named "myFile.txt"

<form action="" method="post" enctype="multipart/form-data">

<input type="file" name="file">

<input type ="submit" value="Submit">

</form>

<?php

echo "File Name: " . $_FILES['file']['name']."
";

echo "File Type : " . $_FILES['file']['type']."
";

echo "File Size : " . $_FILES['file']['size']."
";

echo "Temp Name: " . $_FILES['file']['tmp_name']."
";

echo "Error Info: " . $_FILES['file']['error']. "<br>";

?>

// Output:

[Choose File] myFile.txt   [Submit]

File Name: myFile.txt

File Type : text/plain

File Size : 279

Temp Name: C:\Windows\Temp\php5167.tmp

Error Info: 0

---

file_exists() syntax:

file_exists("myFile.txt")

// Return true if the file exists, return false if not.

e.g.

$f = 'myFile.txt';   // assume that myFile.txt doesn't exist

if (**file_exists($f)**) { echo "The file $f exists"; }

else { echo "The file $f does not exist"; }

// Output: The file myFile.txt does not exist

---

filesize() syntax:

filesize("file.txt")

// Return the size of a file

e.g.

echo **filesize("myFile.txt")**;

// Output: 98

---

file_get_contents() syntax:

file_get_contents("myFile.txt");

// Read the contents of the file.

e.g.

echo **file_get_contents("myFile.txt")**;

// Output: Hi, this is myFile.txt, How are you?

---

file_put_contents() syntax:

file_put_contents("myFile", "contents");

// Write the contents to the file, and return the length.

e.g.

echo **file_put_contents**("myFile.txt", "Hi, this is myFile.txt.");

// Output: 23

---

filter_callback syntax:

FILTER_CALLBACK, array("options"=>function)

// Call a user-defined function or built in function to filter the value.
// FILTER_CALLBACK is the parameter of filter_var()
e.g.

$str="jquery in 8 hours";

echo filter_var($str, **FILTER_CALLBACK,**

array("options"=>"strtoupper")); // call built-in function "strtoupper"

// Output: JQUERY IN 8 HOURS

---

filter_has_var() syntax:

filter_has_var(type, "variable")

// Check if the form input has the specified value
// type: INPUT_GET, INPUT_POST, INPUT_COOKIE, INPUT_SERVER, INPUT_ENV
// variable: an external variable from the form input
e.g.
// assume that we didn't input url in the form

if (!**filter_has_var**(INPUT_POST, "url")){

echo("URL not found");} else {

echo("URL found");}

// Output: URL not found

---

filter_input syntax:

filter_input(type, variable, filter)

// Get an external variable from the form input and filter it.
// type: INPUT_GET, INPUT_POST, INPUT_COOKIE, INPUT_SERVER, INPUT_ENV
// variable: an external variable from the form input
// filter: various filters (see Filter Chart)
e.g.

if(isset($_POST["email"])){ // assume that we input xxx@yyy.com

if(**filter_input**(INPUT_POST, "email", FILTER_VALIDATE_EMAIL)===false){

echo("Email format is not valid"); } else {

```
echo("Email format is valid"); }
}
// Output:   Email format is valid
```

---

filter_input_array() syntax:

filter_input_array(type, $array)

```
// Get multiple external variables from the form input and filter them.
// type: INPUT_GET, INPUT_POST, INPUT_COOKIE, INPUT_SERVER, INPUT_ENV
// $array: multiple external variables from the form input
e.g.
$arr = array (   // assume that we input Ray Yao and 28 in the form
  "name" => array ("filter"=>FILTER_CALLBACK,),
  "age"  => array ( "filter"=>FILTER_VALIDATE_INT,),
);  // "filter" refers to various filters (see Filter Chart)
print_r(filter_input_array(INPUT_POST, $arr));
// Output:
Array(
  [name] => Ray Yao
  [age] => 28
)
```

---

filter_var() syntax:

filter_var($variable, filter)

```
// Filter a variable with the specified filter
// "filter" refers to a built in filter in php. (see Filters Chart)
e.g.
$email = "xxx123@demo.com";
if (filter_var($email, FILTER_VALIDATE_EMAIL))
// FILTER_VALIDATE_EMAIL is a filter to validate email address
{ echo("$email is a valid email address");}
else {echo("$email is not a valid email address");}
// Output:   xxx123@demo.com is a valid email address
```

---

filter_var_array() syntax:

filter_var_array($array)

// Get multiple variables and values.

e.g.

$arr = array(

 'A' => 'Apple',

 'B' => 'Banana',

);

$fruit = **filter_var_array($arr);**

var_dump($fruit);

// Output: array(2){["A"]=>string(5)"Apple" ["B"]=>string(6)"Banana"}

---

final syntax:

final class BaseClass{…}

final public function myFun(){…}

// final class cannot be extended, final function cannot be overridden.

e.g.

<?php

final class BaseClass {

final public function myFun() {

echo "We are final class and final function";

}}

class ChildClass extends BaseClass {   // error

public function myFun() {   // error

echo "Try to extend final class & override final method" ;

}}

?>

// final class cannot be extended, final function cannot be overridden.

---

floatval() syntax:

floatval($data)

// Return a float value

e.g.

$data = "123.456Good!";

echo **floatval($data);**

// Output: 123.456

----

floor() syntax:

floor(number)

// Return a closest integer that is less than or equal to its argument.

e.g.

echo(**floor(9.5)**);

// Output: 9

----

flush() syntax:

flush();

// Push all output to the browser as quick as possible instead of waiting till the whole program has completed, which can speed up the website.

e.g.

<?php

for($num=0; $num<100; $num++){

echo $num;

flush();

}

// assume that there are long long codes in here......

?>

// Output: 12345678......100

----

fopen() syntax:

fopen($filename, mode);

// Open a file in a specified mode. The mode to open a file is:

Mode	Operation
r	open file for reading only, read from the beginning.
w	open file for writing only, clear original content.
a	open file for writing only, append new content.
x	create a new file for writing only.

// Note: If above modes with "+" sign, it means opening the file for both reading and writing. e.g. r+, w+, a+, x+

e.g.

$filename = "myfile.txt";

fopen($filename, r);   // open the file for reading only

fopen($filename, w);   // open the file for writing only

fopen($filename, a+);   // open the file for both writing and reading, append new content to the end when writing.

---

for loop syntax:

for(init, test-expression, increment) { // some codes; **}**

// "init" initializes a variable that is used to control the loop.

// "test-expression" allows to loop if it returns true.

// "increment" will increase 1 after every loop

e.g.

for ($x = 0; $x <= 5; $x++) {   // loop at most 5 times

echo "$x ";

}

// Output: 012345

---

foreach() syntax:

foreach($array as $key=>$value){ }

// foreach() can iterate over all elements of an array.

e.g.

$book=array("A"=>"JSP", "B"=>"ASP", "C"=>"PHP");

foreach ($book as $key => $value){   // iteration

echo "The $key book is about $value.
";

}   // $key stores all keys, $value stores all values

// Output:

The A book is about JSP.

The B book is about ASP.

The C book is about PHP.

---

fprintf() syntax:

fprintf($file," %format", $variable);

// Write a formatted string to a file.

// Replace the %format with the value of $variable

// About %format, please see The String Format Chart.

e.g.

$num = 8; $str = "Hours";

$file = fopen("d:\myFile.txt","w");

fprintf($file,"JAVA in %u %s.", $num, $str);

// $num replaces %u. $str replaces %s

// Please check myFile.txt

// The content of the myFile.txt is: JAVA in 8 Hours

----

fputs() syntax:

// fputs() is an alias of the fwrite(), please see fwrite().

----

fread() syntax:

fread($openfile, length);

// "fread()" reads the content of a file.

// "$openfile" specifies the opened file for reading.

// "length" specifies the maximum number of bytes to read.

e.g.

// Given the content of myfile.txt is: "Hello!"

// the path of the myfile.txt is: D:\myfile.txt

$filename = "D:\myfile.txt";

$openfile = fopen($filename, r);   // open a file with r mode

$content = **fread($openfile, 20)**;   // read 20 bytes

echo "$content";

// Output: Hello!

----

fscanf() syntax:

fscanf($file, "%format");

// Parse a file according to the specified format

// About %format, please see The String Format Chart.

e.g.

// Assume that the contents of myFile.txt is as follows:

   Andy   Student   17

```
$file = fopen("myFile.txt", "r");
$array = fscanf($file, "%s \t %s \t %d");
print_r($array);
// Output:  Array( [0]=>Andy  [1]=>Student  [2]=>17 )
```

---

ftruncate() syntax;

ftruncate($file, size);
// Truncates an open file to the specified size (bytes).
e.g.
```
<?php    // assume that the original file size is 800 bytes.
echo filesize("myFile.txt");    // output file size 800 bytes.
$f = fopen("myFile.txt", "a+");
ftruncate($f,120);    // truncate the file to 120 bytes
fclose($f);
clearstatcache();    // clear cache
echo filesize("myFile.txt");    // check file size again
?>
// Output:  800   120
```

---

function syntax:

function functionName ( ) {......}   // define a function
functionName ( );   // call the function
e.g.
```
<?php
function test( ){    // declare a function
echo ("show a sample");    // output
}
test ( );    // call the function
?>
// Output:  show a sample
```

---

function with argument syntax:

function functionName($argument) {......}   // define a function
functionName(parameter);   // call the function and pass parameter

75

e.g.

```php
<?php
function test( $arg ){   // declare a function with arguments
echo ("$arg");
}
test("display a sample");  // call the function, and pass args.
?>
// Output:  display a sample
```

---

fwrite() syntax:

fwrite($openfile, "contents");

// "fwrite( )" writes the contents to a file.
// "$openfile" specifies the opened file for writing.
// "contents" specifies the contents to write.

e.g.

$filename = "D:\myfile.txt";   // set the path D:\myfile.txt
$openfile = fopen($filename, w);   // open a file with w mode
$content = **fwrite($openfile, "Hello!");**   // writing
echo "Write a file successfully!";
// Output: Write a file successfully!
// If you open D:\myfile.txt, you can see the content "Hello!".

---

getcwd() syntax:

getcwd();

// Return the current working directory.

e.g.

echo **getcwd();**

// Output: /home/phpdirectory

---

getdate() syntax:

getdate();

// Return the information of the local date and time.

e.g.

print_r(getdate());

// Output: Array([seconds]=>26 [minutes]=>38 ..... [year]=>2022)

---

get_resource_type() syntax:

get_resource_type($resource);

// Return the resource type

e.g.

$file = fopen("myFile.txt","r");

echo **get_resource_type**($file);

// Output: stream

---

getenv() syntax:

getenv("VARIABLE");

// Get the value of an environment variable.

e.g.

putenv("USER=Ray Yao");

echo "The user name is: " . **getenv("USER")**;

// Output: The user name is: Ray Yao

---

getFile() syntax:

$e->getFile()

// Output the file in which the exception occurs.

e.g.

try {

throw new Exception("An exception occurs!");

} catch(Exception $e) {

echo "Exception occurs in this file: ".**$e->getFile()**;

}

// Output: Exception occurs in this file: /server/script.php

---

getLine() syntax:

$e->getLine()

// Output the number of the line on which the exception was thrown

e.g.

try {

throw new Exception("An error occurs!");
} catch(Exception $e) {
  echo "Exception occurs in this line: ".**$e->getLine()**;
}
// Output: Exception occurs in this line: 3

---

getMessage() syntax:
$e->getMessage()
// Output the exception message.
e.g.
try {
  throw new Exception("An exception occurs!");
} catch(Exception $e) {
  echo $**e->getMessage()**;
}
// Output: An exception occurs!

---

global variable syntax:
$variable=value;   function funName(){ global $variable }
// A global variable is declared outside the function, it can be used in everywhere;
// If a global variable is used inside a function, the variable should be prefixed a keyword "global"
e.g.
<?php
$x = 100; $y = 200;   // global variable
function myFun(){
global $x, $y;   // use two global variables inside a function
$y = $x + $y;
echo $y;
}
myFun();
?>
// Output: 200

---

gmdate() syntax:

gmdate(format, timestamp)

// Format the local GMT/UTC date/time in the specified format.

// About data/time format, please see Data Time Format Chart.

e.g.

echo **gmdate("Y F jS l h:i:s a");**

// Output: 2022 November 16th Wednesday 06:08:20 pm

---

gmmktime() syntax:

gmmktime(hour, minute, second, month, day, year)

// Return the Unix timestamp for the given GMT date.

e.g.

echo date("M-d-Y", **gmmktime(0, 0, 0, 1, 1, 2018))." ";**
echo date("M-d-Y", **gmmktime(0, 0, 0, 10, 10, 2022)**);

// Output: Jan-01-2018   Oct-10-2022

---

header syntax;

header("string_to_send");

// Send a HTTP header to a client before some other outputs

e.g.

header('Location: url');

 // Redirect the current web page to another web page.

header("Cache-Control: no_cache");

// Indicate that browser must always reload this page without cache.

header("HTTP/1.0 404 Not Found");

// Set HTTP Status in the header response.

e.g.

<?php

header("Location:http://www.amazon.com");   // to Amazon

?>

// Output: (We can see the home page of Amazon)

---

heredoc syntax:

$var= <<<EOF

texts

EOF;

// Heredoc is a way to write large amounts of text in PHP code without the single quote, double quote delimiters.

// Heredoc starts with <<<EOF and ends with EOF; End tag must have no indentation or spaces, and must have a semicolon.

e.g.

$book="C# in 8 Hours";

$var= <<<EOF

The book is: $book

EOF;

echo $var;

// Output: The book is: C# in 8 Hours

---

htmlentities() syntax:

htmlentities($characters)

// Convert characters to html entities

e.g.

$str = '<a href="https://www.amazon.com">Amazon</a>';

echo **htmlentities($str);**

// Output: <a href="https://www.amazon.com">Amazon</a>

---

html_entity_decode() syntax:

html_entity_decode($html_entities);

// Convert html entities to characters.

e.g.

$str = '<a href="https://www.amazon.com">Amazon</a>';

echo **html_entity_decode($str);**

// Output: <a href="https://www.amazon.com">Amazon</a>

---

htmlspecialchars() syntax:

htmlspecialchars($predefined_characters);

// Convert predefined characters to html entitles.

// About predefined characters, please see Predefined Chars Chart

e.g.

$str = 'Here is a "<i>italic</i>" text.';

echo **htmlspecialchars($str);**

// Output: Here is a "<i>italic</i>" text.

----

htmlspecialchars_decode() syntax:

htmlspecialchars_decode($html_entities);

// Convert html entities to predefined characters.

// About predefined characters, please see Predefined Chars Chart

e.g.

$str = 'Here is a "<i>italic</i>" text.';

echo **htmlspecialchars_decode($str);**

// Output: Here is a "<i>italic</i>" text.

----

http_build_query() syntax:

http_build_query($data)

// Generate a URL-encoded query string from an array.

e.g.

$data=array("a"=>"ant", "b"=>"bee", "c"=>"cat", "d"=>"dog");

echo **http_build_query($data)**;

// Output: a=ant&b=bee&c=cat&d=dog

----

iconv() syntax:

iconv($input_charset, $output_charset, $str);

// Convert a string to requested character encoding.

e.g.

$str = " EURO '€' ";

echo 'Original :', ("$str"), PHP_EOL;

echo 'Translated :', **iconv("UTF-8", "ISO-8859-1//TRANSLIT", $str)**;

// Output:

Original : EURO '€'

Translated : EURO 'EUR'

---

if statement syntax:

if (test-expression) {   // if true do this;   **}**

// "if statement" executes codes inside { ... } only if a specified condition is true, does not execute any codes inside {...} if the condition is false.

e.g.

$x = 200; $y = 100;

if ($x > $y){   // if true, run following code

echo "x is greater than y.";

}

// Output: x is greater than y.

---

if-else Statement syntax:

if (test-expression){   // if true do this;   **}**

else { // if false do this;   **}**

// "if...else statement" runs a part of codes if the test returns true or runs other part of codes if the test returns false.

e.g.

<?php

$x = 100; $y = 200;

if ($x > $y){   // if true, run this code block

echo "x is greater than y.";

}

else {   // if false, run this code block

echo "x is less than y";

}

?>

// Output: x is less than y

---

if...elseif...else syntax:

if (condition){ // if_true_do_this }

elseif(condition){ // otherwise, if_true_do_this }

else{ // if_false_do_this }

e.g.

```
$h=date("H");
```
if ($h<"11"){ echo "Good morning!"; }
elseif ($h<"19"){ echo "Good day!"; }
else{ echo "Good night!"; }
// Output: Good morning!

---

implode() syntax:

implode(separator, $array)
// Join array elements with a string
e.g.
```
$arr = array('Scala' , 'in' , '8' , 'Hours');
```
echo **implode(" * ", $arr);**
// Output: Scala * in * 8 * Hours

---

in_array() syntax:

in_array("element", $arr)
// Return true if the specified element is in the array, return false if not.
e.g.
```
$arr = array("ant", "bee", "cat", "dog");
```
if (**in_array("cat", $arr)**){
echo "The 'cat' is in the array";
}
// Output: The 'cat' is in the array

---

include() syntax:

include("anotherFile.php")
// Import the code from another.php to the current file
// "include()" is usually in the middle of the file, if the program has an error, a message will appear, but the program will keep going.
e.g.
1.   <!--file1.php-->
<?php   echo " From file1.php "; ?>
2.   <!--file2.php-->
<?php

echo " From file2.php ";

include("file1.php");   // import file1.php to here

?>

// Output: From file2.php   From file1.php

----

include_once() syntax:

include_once("anotherFile.php")

// Import the code from another.php to the current file for only once.

// "include_once()" is usually in the middle of the file, if the program has an error, a message will appear, but the program will keep going.

e.g.

1. <!--file1.php-->

<?php   echo " From file1.php "; ?>

2. <!--file2.php-->

<?php

echo " From file2.php ";

include_once("file1.php");   // import file1.php to here once

?>

// Output: From file2.php   From file1.php

----

insert into table syntax:

INSERT INTO tableName (fieldnames) VALUES ('data')

// Add new records to a MySQL table by inserting data

// Note: In the PHP code, if we use MySQL command to insert strings into a table, the strings should be enclosed by \" symbols.

e.g.

```
<?php
$con=new mysqli("servername","username","password","db");
if ($con->connect_error) {   // check connection
die("Connection fails: " . $con->connect_error);
}
echo "Connection succeeds";
?>
```

```
$sql = "INSERT INTO myTable (firstname, lastname) VALUES
(\"Andy\", \"Smith\")";
if ($con->query($sql) === TRUE) {
  echo "Insert data successfully";
}
?>
```
// Output: Connection succeeds   Insert data successfully

---

insert into table syntax:

$sql="insert into tableName (columns) values ("data")";
$query=mysqli_query($con, $sql);   // execute the query
// $sql="insert into tableName (columns) value ("data")" is used to insert data into a table. Note: In the PHP code, if we use MySQL command to insert strings into a table, the strings should be enclosed by \" symbols.
// "$con" is the connection to MySql server. (see mysqli_connect()).
e.g.
```
<?php
$con= mysqli_connect( "localhost", "root", "12345678" );
if( $con ) {     // if connect MySQL server successfully
echo " Connect successfully! ";
}
$select=mysqli_select_db( $con, "myDB" );
if( $select ) {   // if select database "myDB" successfully
echo " Select myDB successfully!<br> ";
}     // assume that myDB has a table "colortable"
$sql="insert into colortable (color1, color2, color3, color4) values
(\"pink\",\"navy\",\"purple\",\"orange\")";
// insert four strings data into the four columns of the table
$query=mysqli_query( $con, $sql );   // execute query
if( $query ) {
echo "Insert data successfully! ";
}
?>
```
// Output:

Connect successfully! Select myDB successfully!
Insert data successfully!

----

insert into table syntax:

insert into TableName (field1, field2, field3, …)
values (value1, value2, value3, …);
// Insert data to a table in a database
e.g.
use library;
insert into books(title, price, author)
values("Java", 13.99, "Ray Yao");
insert into books(title, price, author)
values("Html", 12.88, "Ann Lee");
insert into books(title, price, author)
values("Lamp", 11.67, "Jan Poe");
// "insert into books(title, price, author) values("Java", 13.99, "Ray Yao");" will insert three values "Java", 13.99, "Ray Yao" into associated three fields "title, price, author".
// Three records are being inserted to a table "books" in the "library".

----

intdiv() syntax:

intdiv(num1, num2)
// num1 divides num2, and convert the result to an integer
e.g.
var_dump(**intdiv(100, 33)**);
// Output: 3

----

interface syntax:

interface interfaceName{method();}
class ClassName implements InterfaceName{method(){}}
// With interfaces, you can specify which methods a class must implement, Interfaces are defined by the interface keyword.
// A class can implement the interface. Interface method has no body.
// The method of the class can override the method of the interface.

e.g.
```php
<?php
interface Animal {    // define an interface
  public function roar();    // define a method with body
}
class Dog implements Animal {    // implement the interface
  public function roar() {
    echo "WOW, WOW, WOW";
}}
$d = new Dog();
$d->roar();
?>
// Output:   WOW, WOW, WOW
```

---

is_dir() syntax:

is_dir($variable)

// Return true if the $variable is a directory.

e.g.

```php
$d = "d:\myFolder";
if (is_dir($d)){ echo ("$d a directory.");}
// Output:   myFolder is a directory.
```

---

is_file() syntax:

is_file($variable)

// Return true if the $variable is a file.

e.g.

```php
$f = "myFile.txt";
if(is_file($f)) { echo ("$f is a file.");}
// Output:   myFile.txt is a file.
```

---

is_int() syntax:

is_int($variable)

// Return true if the $variable is an integer.

e.g.

```
$num = 168;
if(is_int($num)){ echo "$num is an integer.";}
```
// Output: 168 is an integer.

---

is_integer() syntax:

// is_integer is an alias of in_int(), please see is_int().

---

is_null() syntax:

is_null($variable)

// Return true if the $variable is null.

e.g.

```
$var1 = null; if(is_null($var1)){ echo " var1 is null. ";}
$var2 = NULL; if(is_null($var2)){ echo " var2 is null. ";}
```
// Output: var1 is null.   var2 is null.

---

is_numeric() syntax:

is_numeric($variable)

// Return true if the $variable is a numeric string or a number.

e.g.

```
$var = "168";
if(is_numeric($var)){ echo "$var is a numeric string or a number";}
```
// Output: 168 is a numeric string or a number

---

is_readable() syntax:

is_readable($variable)

// Return true if the $variable is a readable file.

e.g.

```
$f = "myFile.txt";
if(is_readable($f)) { echo ("$f is a readable file.");}
```
// Output: myFile.txt is a readable file.

---

is_string() syntax:

is_string($variable)

// Return true if the $variable is a string.

e.g.

$var = "CHARACTERS";

if(**is_string($var)**){ echo "$var is a string.";}

// Output: CHARACTERS is a string.

---

isset() syntax:

isset($variable)

// Return true if the $variable is set a value, return false if not.

e.g.

$var = 10;

if (**isset($var)**) {   // return true if $var is set a value

echo "The var is set";

}

// Output: The var is set

---

is_executable() syntax:

is_executable($file)

// Return true if the $file is executable.

e.g.

$f = "config.exe";

if(**is_executable($f)**){echo ("$f is executable.");}

// Output: config.exe is executable.

---

is_writable() syntax:

is_writable($variable)

// Return true if the $variable is a writable file.

e.g.

$f = "myFile.txt";

if(**is_writable($f)**) { echo ("$f is a writable file.");}

// Output: myFile.txt is a writable file.

---

is_writeable() syntax:

// is_writeable() is an alias of is_writable(), please see is_writable()

---

json_decode() syntax:

json_decode($json, bool)

// Convert a JSON encoded object into a PHP variable

// If "bool" arg is true, convert an json format to an array format.

e.g.

$json = '{"a":6, "b":3, "c":8}';

var_dump(**json_decode($json, true**));

// Output: array(3){ ["a"]=>int(6) ["b"]=>int(3) ["c"]=>int(8) }

---

json_encode() syntax:

json_encode($variable)

// Encode a variable value to JSON format

e.g.

$age = array("Andy"=>19, "Bob"=>16, "Caddie"=>18);

echo **json_encode**($age);

// Output: {"Andy":19, "Bob":16, "Caddie":18}

---

key() syntax:

key($array)

// Return the element key of an array according to the current position of the internal pointer. The default position of the key is 0.

e.g.

$arr=array("A","B","C","D");

echo "The key of the current position is: " . **key($arr)**;

// Output: The key of the current position is: 0

---

krsort() syntax:

krsort($array)

// Sorts an associative array keys in descending order

e.g.

$score=array("Rosy"=>"90","Andy"=>"100","Jony"=>"85");

krsort($score);   // sort keys

print_r($score);

// Output: Array([Rosy] => 90   [Jony] => 85   [Andy] => 100)

---

ksort() syntax:

ksort($array)

// Sorts an associative array keys in ascending order.

e.g.

$score=array("Rosy"=>"90","Andy"=>"100","Jony"=>"85");

ksort($score);   // sort keys

print_r($score);

// Output: Array([Andy] => 100   [Jony] => 85   [Rosy] => 90)

---

less / more than syntax:

where FieldName less/more than value;

// Select records less/more than a specified value in a table.

e.g.

1. Given the current status of the table "books" as follows.

use library;

select * from books;

```
+----+-------+---------+-------+-------+---------+
| id | title | writer  | pages | price | publish |
+----+-------+---------+-------+-------+---------+
|  1 | Java  | Ray Yao |   200 | 13.99 |    2018 |
|  2 | Ajax  | Ann Lee |   190 | 12.88 |    2019 |
|  3 | Html  | Jan Poe |   110 | 10.99 |    2014 |
|  4 | Ruby  | Ray Yao |   200 | 13.99 |    2017 |
|  5 | Rust  | R.Y.    |   128 | 12.99 |    2016 |
|  6 | Node  | R.Y.    |   128 | 12.99 |    2020 |
|  7 | Lamp  | Jan Poe |   120 | 11.67 |    2015 |
+----+-------+---------+-------+-------+---------+
```

2. Show filtered data by using "<="

select * from books **where** price <= 12.00;

```
+----+-------+---------+-------+-------+---------+
| id | title | writer  | pages | price | publish |
+----+-------+---------+-------+-------+---------+
|  3 | Html  | Jan Poe |   110 | 10.99 |    2014 |
|  7 | Lamp  | Jan Poe |   120 | 11.67 |    2015 |
+----+-------+---------+-------+-------+---------+
```

// "where price <= 12.00;" shows the price less than or equal to 12.00.

// (You can try ">=" operator by yourself).

---

limit records syntax:

$sql = "SELECT * FROM Orders LIMIT records";

// Specify how many records to return.

e.g.

$sql = "SELECT * FROM Orders **LIMIT 50**";

// Specify 1- 50 records to return

$sql = "SELECT * FROM Orders **LIMIT 5 OFFSET 10**";

// Specify 5 records to return, start from 11

---

list() syntax:

list($a, $b, $c, $d, …) = $array;

// Assign multiple values to multiple variables at a time by an array.

e.g.

$arr = array("Ant", "Bee", "Cat", "Dog");

list($a, $b, $c, $d) = $arr;

echo "$a, $b, $c, $d";

// Output: Ant, Bee, Cat, Dog

---

local variable syntax:

function funName(){ $variable=value; }

// A local variable is declared inside the function, it is only used inside current function.

e.g.

```
<?php
$num=200;   // This $num is a global variable.
function test( ){
$num=100;   // This $num is a local variable.
echo $num;
}
test();
?>
```

// Output: 100

---

log() syntax:

log(number)

// Return the natural logarithm of a number

e.g.

echo(**log(10)**." ");   echo(**log(1)**." ");

// Output: 2.302585092994   0

---

ltrim() syntax:

ltrim($string, $substring)

// Remove the spaces or substring from the left side of a string

e.g.

$str = "Hi, Friends";

echo **ltrim**($str, "Hi,");   // remove Hi,

// Output: Friends

---

mail() syntax:

mail(to, subject, message, headers, parameters);

// Send an email

to	Specify email recipient.
subject	Specify email subject
message	Specify email content. Separate lines with LF(\n).
headers	(optional) From, Cc, and Bcc. Separate with CRLF(\r\n)
parameters	(optional) Specify additional parameters for the mail sender.

// Email content must not exceed 70 characters per line.

e.g.

```
<?php
$msg = "email_text";   // the email contents
mail("person@demo.com", "subject", $msg);   // send email
?>
```

---

max() syntax:

max(num1, num2, num3,...);

// Return the largest value among numbers.

e.g.

echo(**max(1,3,5,7,9)**);

// Output: 9

---

md5() syntax:

md5($string, bool);

// Generate the MD5 hash of a string. If "bool" is true, generate 16 binary chars, if "bool" is false (default), generate 32 hex chars.

e.g.

$str = "Good";

echo **md5($str)**;   // generate 32 hex characters by default

// Output: 0c6ad70beb3a7e76c3fc7adab7c46acc

---

md5_file() syntax:

md5_file($file);

// Generate the MD5 hash of a file.

e.g.

$f="myFile.txt";

echo **md5_file($f)**;

// Output: 2aa71b9b39feee485ace2843c0d0bfbb

---

microtime() syntax:

microtime()

// Return the current Unix timestamp with microseconds

e.g.

echo(**microtime()**);

// Output: 0.51976200 1668780938

---

min() syntax:

min(num1, num2, num3,…);

// Return the smallest value among numbers.

e.g.

echo(**min(1,3,5,7,9)**);

// Output: 1

---

mkdir() syntax:

mkdir("path/directory/", permission)

// Create a directory with specified permissions, return 1 if successfully.

// About permission, please see Permissions Chart.

e.g.

mkdir("/php/myFolder/", 0770);   // return 0 if fail
// permissions to the owner and the owner's user group
// Output: 1

---

mktime() syntax:
mktime($hour, $minute, $second, $month, $day, $year)
// Return a Unix timestamp (seconds) from Unix Epoch (1-1-1970) to the specified date and time. All parameters are optional.
e.g.
<?php   // Return an Unix timestamp from Unix Epoch to current time
print(**mktime()**);
?>
// Output: 1668797908

---

move_uploaded_file() syntax:
bool move_uploaded_file($file_tmp_name, $destination)
// Move an uploaded file with temporary name to new location.
e.g.
move_uploaded_file($_FILES["file"]["tmp_name"], "upload/".
$_FILES["file"]["name"]);
// Move FILES["file"]["tmp_name"] to "upload" folder, the new file name becomes $_FILES["file"]["name"]).

---

mt_rand() syntax:
mt_rand(min, max)
// Generate a random number from min to max. Arguments are optional.
e.g.
echo(**mt_rand()**." "); echo(**mt_rand(100,1000)**);
// Output: 2045534323   168

---

mysqli_affected_rows() syntax:
mysqli_affected_rows()
// Return the number of affected rows from the query.

e.g.

$con=new mysqli("servername","username","password","db");

$sql = "DELETE FROM myTable WHERE id < 6";

mysql_query($sql, $con);

$rc = **mysqli_affected_rows()**;

echo "Records deleted: " . $rc;

mysql_close($con);

// Records deleted: 5

---

mysqli_close( ) syntax:

mysqli_close( );

// Close a previously opened database connection

e.g.

$con= mysqli_connect("localhost", "root", "12345678");

mysqli_close($con);   // close the connection

echo "The connection is closed successfully!";

// Output:

The connection is closed successfully!

---

mysqli_connect() syntax:

mysqli_connect("host", "username", "password");

// "mysqli_connect( ) lets PHP connect MySql server.

// "host": specifies a host name or an IP address

// "username": specifies a MySql user name.

// "password": specifies a MySql password.

e.g.

$con = **mysqli_connect("localhost", "root", "12345678");**

if($con) {   // if connect MySQL server successfully

echo " Connect successfully! ";

}

// Output: Connect successfully!

---

mysqli_connect_error() syntax:

mysqli_connect_error()

// Return the message of the connection error with MySQL

e.g.

```
$conn = mysqli_connect("server", "user", "password", "db");
if (!$conn) {
    die("Connection failed: " . mysqli_connect_error());
}
```

// Output: Connection failed: php_network_getaddresses: getaddrinfo failed: No such host is known.

---

mysqli_data_seek() syntax:

mysqli_data_seek($result, row);

// Move the pointer to an arbitrary row in the result-set.

// "row" parameter starts from row 0.

e.g.

```
$con=new mysqli("servername","username","password","db");
$sql="SELECT * FROM myTable";
if ($result=mysqli_query($con, $sql)){
    mysqli_data_seek($result, 5);   // Seek to row 5
}
```

// Point to row 5 in the result set.

---

mysqli_error() syntax:

mysqli_error($con);

// Returns the description of the last error.

e.g.

```
$con=new mysqli("servername","username","password","db");
mysqli_query($con, "SELECT * FORM myTable");
$error = mysqli_error($con);   // Error
print("Error Found: ".$error);
```

// Output: Error Found: You have an error in your SQL syntax; ......

---

mysqli_fetch_array() syntax:

$array=mysqli_fetch_array($query)

// "mysqli_fetch_array( )" returns an indexed and associative array that contains rows of a table. The element keys can be both number type and string type. For example: [number]=>value   [string]=>value.

e.g.

```php
<?php
$con= mysqli_connect( "localhost", "root", "12345678" );
if( $con ) {     // if connect MySQL server successfully
echo " Connect successfully! ";
}
$select=mysqli_select_db( $con, "myDB" );
if( $select ) {    // if select database "myDB" successfully
echo " Select myDB successfully!<br> ";
}    // assume that myDB has a table "colortable"
$sql="select * from colortable";  // "*" represents all columns
$query=mysqli_query( $con, $sql);
while ( $array=mysqli_fetch_array($query) ){   // return an array
print_r($array);  // print_r( ) is used to print the array
echo "<br>";
}
?>
```

// Output:

Connect successfully! Select myDB successfully!

```
Array (
[0] => 1              [id] => 1
[1] => red            [color1] => red
[2] => yellow         [color2] => yellow
[3] => green          [color3] => green
[4] => blue           [color4] => blue
[5] => sky            [color5] => sky
)
```

---

mysqli_fetch_assoc() syntax:

$array=mysqli_fetch_assoc($query)

// "mysqli_fetch_assoc( )" returns an assoc array that contains rows of a table. Its element key is always a string type. e.g. [string]=> value.
e.g.
```php
<?php
$con= mysqli_connect( "localhost", "root", "12345678" );
if( $con ) {     // if connect MySQL server successfully
echo " Connect successfully! ";
}
$select=mysqli_select_db( $con, "myDB" );
if( $select ) {    // if select database "myDB" successfully
echo " Select myDB successfully!<br> ";
}    // assume that myDB has a table "colortable"
$sql="select * from colortable";  // "*" represents all columns
$query=mysqli_query( $con, $sql);
while ( $array=mysqli_fetch_assoc($query) ){    // return an array
print_r($array);  // print_r( ) is used to print the array
echo "<br>";
}
?>
```
// Output:
Connect successfully! Select myDB successfully!
Array ([id] => 1   [color1] => red   [color2] => yellow   [color3] => green   [color4] => blue   [color5] => sky)
Array ([id] => 2   [color1] => pink   [color2] => navy   [color3] => purple   [color4] => orange   [color5] => olive)

---

mysqli_fetch_row() syntax:

$array=mysqli_fetch_row($query)

// "mysqli_fetch_row( )" returns an indexed array that contains rows of a table. Its element key is always a number type. e.g. [number]=> value.
e.g.
```php
<?php
$con= mysqli_connect( "localhost", "root", "12345678" );
if( $con ) {     // if connect MySQL server successfully
```

```php
echo " Connect successfully! ";
}
$select=mysqli_select_db( $con, "myDB" );
if( $select ) {    // if select database "myDB" successfully
echo " Select myDB successfully!<br> ";
}   // assume that myDB has a table "colortable"
$sql="select * from colortable";  // "*" represents all columns
$query=mysqli_query( $con, $sql);
while ( $array=mysqli_fetch_row($query) ){    // return an array
print_r($array);  // print_r( ) is used to print the array
echo "<br>";
}
?>
```

// Output:

Connect successfully! Select myDB successfully!

Array ([0] => 1 [1] => red [2] => yellow [3] => green [4] => blue [5] => sky)

Array ([0] => 2 [1] => pink [2] => navy [3] => purple [4] => orange [5] => olive)

---

mysqli_free_result() syntax:

mysqli_free_result($result)

// Release the memory related to the result, return true if succeed.

e.g.

$result = mysqli_query($con, "SELECT * FORM myTable");

var_dump(**mysqli_free_result($result)**);

// Output: bool(true)

---

mysqli_get_server_info() syntax:

$version = mysqli_get_server_info($con);

// Return the version of the MySQL server.

e.g.

$con = mysqli_connect("server", "user", "password", "db");

$version = **mysqli_get_server_info($con)**;

// Output: MySQL Server Version: 5.7.12-log

---

mysqli_num_rows() syntax:

$total_numbers = mysqli_num_rows($result);

// Return the number of rows in a result set.

e.g.

$con = mysqli_connect("server", "user", "password", "db");

$sql="SELECT * FROM myTable ";

$result=mysqli_query($con, $sql) ;

$rowNum=**mysqli_num_rows($result)**;

var_dump($rowNum); // assume that there are 10 records in result

// Output: int(10)

---

mysqli_query() syntax:

mysqli_query($queryVariable, $connectVariable);

// Execute the query

e.g.

$con=mysqli_connect("servername","username","password","db");

if (!$con) { die('Fail to connect! '); }

$sql = "SELECT * FROM Mytable";

mysqli_query($sql, $con);   // run the query

echo "Select data successfully!";

mysqli_close($con);

// Output: Select data successfully!

---

mysqli_real_escape_string() syntax:

mysqli_real_escape_string($string)

// Escape special characters in a string, making it legal to use in SQL.

e.g.

mysqli_connect("server", "user", "password", "db");

$sql="SELECT * FROM myTable ";

var_dump(**mysql_real_escape_string($sql)**);

// Output: string(25) "SELECT * FROM \'myTable\'"

---

mysqli_result() syntax:

mysqli_result($result, row, column)

// Return the value in a cell according to the specified row and column in a table.

e.g.

var_dump(**mysql_result($result, 0, name)**);

var_dump(**mysql_result($result, 1, 'name')**);

// Output:

string(3) "Alf"

string(3) "Bob"

----

mysqli_select_db() syntax:

mysqli_select_db($con, "databaseName");

// Select a database to connect a server.

// "$con" is the connection to MySql server. (See mysqli_connect( )).

// "databaseName" specifies the name of the database.

e.g.

```php
<?php
$con= mysqli_connect( "localhost", "root", "12345678" );
if( $con ) {    // if connect MySQL server successfully
echo  " Connect successfully! ";
}
$select=mysqli_select_db( $con, "myDB" );
if( $select ) {    // if select database "myDB" successfully
echo  " Select myDB successfully!<br> ";
}
?>
```

// Output: Connect successfully!   Select myDB successfully!

----

namespace syntax:

namespace MyNamespace;

// Namespace can avoid the conflict of two class names, two function names, and two variable names, and two constant names.

e.g.

namespace MyNameSpace1;   // define the 1st namespace

```
class MyClass {...}
const DEMO = "Nice!";
function myFun() { ... }
```
namespace MyNameSpace2;   // define the 2nd namespace
```
class MyClass {...}
const DEMO = "Good!";
function myFun() { ... }
```
// In this example, two class names, two constant names, two function names are the same, however the names of two namespaces are different, therefore, which can resolve the problem of name conflict.

---

natcasesort() syntax:

natcasesort($array)

// Sort the array values by using a "natural order" algorithm.

// natcasesort() is case insensitive

e.g.

$arr = array("a26.jpg", "a45.jpg", "A18.jpg", "A32.jpg");

natcasesort($arr);   // case insensitive

print_r($arr);

// Output: Array([2] => A18.jpg   [0] => a26.jpg   [1] => A32.jpg   [3] => a45.jpg)

---

natsort() syntax:

natsort($array)

// Sort the array values by using a "natural order" algorithm.

// natsort() is case sensitive.

e.g.

$arr = array("a26.jpg", "a45.jpg", "A18.jpg", "A32.jpg");

natsort($arr);   // case sensitive

print_r($arr);

// Output: Array([2] => A18.jpg   [3] => A32.jpg   [0] => a26.jpg   [1] => a45.jpg)

---

next() syntax:

next($array)

// Return the next element value to which the pointer points.

e.g.

$arr = array("ant", "bee", "cat", "dog");

echo current($arr)." ";   // current element value

echo **next($arr);**   // next element value

// Output: ant   bee

---

nl2br() syntax:

nl2br("string");

// Insert <br/> where all \n occur in the string

e.g.

echo **nl2br**("The first line \n The second line");

// Output: The first line

         The second line

---

not equal syntax:

where FieldName != value;

// Select some data that is not equal to a specific value.

e.g.

1. Given the current status of the table "books" as follows:

use library;

select * from books;

```
+----+-------+---------+-------+-------+---------+
| id | title | writer  | pages | price | publish |
+----+-------+---------+-------+-------+---------+
|  1 | Java  | Ray Yao |  200  | 13.99 |  2018   |
|  2 | Ajax  | Ann Lee |  190  | 12.88 |  2019   |
|  3 | Html  | Jan Poe |  110  | 10.99 |  2014   |
|  4 | Ruby  | Ray Yao |  200  | 13.99 |  2017   |
|  5 | Rust  | R.Y.    |  128  | 12.99 |  2016   |
|  6 | Node  | R.Y.    |  128  | 12.99 |  2020   |
|  7 | Lamp  | Jan Poe |  120  | 11.67 |  2015   |
+----+-------+---------+-------+-------+---------+
```

2. Show filtered data by using "!="

select * from books **where** writer **!=** "R.Y.";

```
+----+-------+---------+-------+-------+---------+
| id | title | writer  | pages | price | publish |
+----+-------+---------+-------+-------+---------+
|  1 | Java  | Ray Yao |   200 | 13.99 |    2018 |
|  2 | Ajax  | Ann Lee |   190 | 12.88 |    2019 |
|  3 | Html  | Jan Poe |   110 | 10.99 |    2014 |
|  4 | Ruby  | Ray Yao |   200 | 13.99 |    2017 |
|  7 | Lamp  | Jan Poe |   120 | 11.67 |    2015 |
+----+-------+---------+-------+-------+---------+
```

// "where writer != "R.Y.";" shows the filtered data except the writer who is R. Y.

---

null value syntax:

$var = null

// A null value indicates that the variable has no value.

// Null can clear the data of a variable.

e.g.

$var="Hi, my friend!";

$var=null;

var_dump($var);

// Output: Null

---

number_format() syntax:

number_format(number, decimals)

// Format a number with grouped thousands.

e.g.

echo **number_format**("8888888", 2);

// Output: 8,888,888.00

---

ob_clean() syntax:

ob_clean();

// Clean the current contents in the output buffer. Buffer is not closed.

e.g.

ob_start();   echo "This output will not be seen";

ob_clean();

// ob_clean() stops sending buffer contents to the browser.

---

ob_end_clean() syntax:

ob_end_clean();

// Clean the current contents in the output buffer, then close buffer.

e.g.

ob_start();   echo "This output will not be seen";

ob_end_clean();

// ob_end_clean() stops sending buffer contents to the browser.

---

ob_end_flush() syntax:

ob_end_flush()

// Send the output buffer contents to the browser, then close the buffer.

e.g.

ob_start();   echo "This output can be seen";

ob_end_flush();

// Output: This output can be seen.

---

ob_flush() syntax:

ob_flush()

// Send the output buffer contents to the browser. Buffer is not closed.

e.g.

ob_start();   echo "This output can be seen";

ob_flush();

// Output: This output can be seen.

---

ob_get_clean() syntax:

ob_get_clean()

// Store the output buffer contents to a variable, then close the buffer.

e.g.

ob_start();

echo 'I will be stored in a variable';

$variable = **ob_get_clean();**   // buffer is now closed

echo "Variable value : $variable";

// Output: Variable value : I will be stored in a variable

---

ob_get_flush() syntax:

ob_get_flush()

// Send the output buffer contents to the browser, and store the output buffer contents to a variable, then close the buffer.

e.g.

ob_start();

echo "I will be stored in a variable. \n";

$variable = **ob_get_flush();**   // buffer is now closed

echo "Variable value : $variable";

// Output: I will be stored in a variable.
   Variable value : I will be stored in a variable.

---

ob_get_contents() syntax:

ob_get_contents()

// Send the output buffer contents to the browser, and store the output buffer contents to a variable. The buffer is not closed.

e.g.

ob_start();

echo "I will be stored in a variable. \n";

$variable = **ob_get_contents();**   // buffer is not closed

echo "Variable value : $variable";

// Output: I will be stored in a variable.
   Variable value : I will be stored in a variable.

---

ob_get_length()

ob_get_length()

// Get the length of the output buffer contents

e.g.

ob_start();

echo "R in 8 Hours";   // 12 characters

$length = **ob_get_length();**

echo "\n"."The length of the output buffer contents: $length ";

// Output: R in 8 Hours
   The length of the output buffer content: 12

---

ob_get_level() syntax:

ob_get_level()

// Return the nesting level of the active output buffers, return 0 if inactive.

e.g.

ob_start();

$buf_level = **ob_get_level()**;   echo " Buffer level: $buf_level ";

ob_start();

$buf_level = **ob_get_level()**;   echo " Buffer level: $buf_level ";

ob_start();

$buf_level = **ob_get_level()**;   echo " Buffer level: $buf_level ";

Output: Buffer level: 1   Buffer level: 2   Buffer level: 3

----

ob_start() syntax:

ob_start()

// Start an output buffer, which stores the contents to output.

e.g.

ob_start();   echo "This output can be seen";

ob_end_flush();   // close the buffer

// Output: This output can be seen

----

object syntax:

$object = new class-name;   // create an object

$object->variable;   // an object references a property

$object->functionName( );   // an object references a method

// Object is an instance of a class.

e.g.

<?php

class MyClass{   // define a class

var $p = "A class & object example ";   // define a variable "$p"

}

$obj= new MyClass();   // create an object "obj"

echo $obj -> p;   // an object references a variable

?>

// Output: A class & object example

---

order by syntax:

SELECT columnName FROM tableName ORDER BY columnName ASC|DESC

// Sort the records in ascending order or in descending order

e.g.

$sql = "SELECT id, firstname, lastname FROM myTable **ORDER BY firstName DESC**";

// Sort the firstName in descending order

---

overloading syntax:

function __call($name, $arg){...}

// Different object calls a method with same name and with different parameter, which is called overloading.

// __call() can implement method overloading

// __call() is invoked when an inexistent function is called.

// $funName is the function name, $arg is an array parameter.

e.g.

e.g.

```
<?php
class MyClass {
function __call($name, $arg){   // overloading
return $arg[0] + $arg[1];
}}
$obj1 = new MyClass();
echo $obj1->sum(10)." ";     // call __call()
$obj2 = new MyClass();
echo $obj2->sum(20,30)." ";  // call __call()
?>
// Output:  10  50
```

---

override syntax:

class BaseClass{function myFun(){...}}

class DerivedClass extends BaseClass{function myFun(){...}}

// The method of the base class and the method of the derived class owe the same name and same parameter, which is called overriding.
// Overriding means that the method of the derived class overrides the method of the base class.

e.g.

```php
<?php
class Class1{
public function show(){    // the method of the base class
return ' Class1 Information  ';
}}
class Class2 extends Class1{
public function show(){    // the method of the base class
return ' Class2 Message  ';
}}
$obj1 = new Class1();
echo $obj1->show();
$obj2 = new Class2();
echo $obj2->show();
// Output:   Class1 Information     Class2 Message
```

-----

parent::__construct() syntax:

parent::__construct();

// In derived class, call the constructor of the base class.

e.g.

```php
<?php
class BaseClass {
function __construct() {
print "I am the constructor of base class" . PHP_EOL;
}}
class DerivedClass extends BaseClass {
function __construct() {
parent::__construct();  // call the constructor of BaseClass
}}
$obj = new DerivedClass();
```

?>
// Output: I am the constructor of base class

---

parse_str() syntax:

parse_str("string", $array);
// Parse a string to an array

e.g.

parse_str(" flower=rose & color=red ", $array);
print_r($array);
// Output: Array([flower] => rose   [color] => red)

PHP_EOL syntax:

echo PHP_EOL;   // Enter new line

e.g.

echo "Hello world!";
echo PHP_EOL;   // enter new line
echo "Hi, my friend!";
// Output:
Hello world!
Hi, my friend!

---

phpinfo() syntax:

phpinfo();
// Return information about PHP's installation and configuration.

e.g.

phpinfo()
// Output information about PHP version, variables modules, server…

---

pi() syntax:

pi();
// Return as approximate value of pi.

e.g.

echo(**pi()**);
// Output: 3.1415926535898

---

polymorphism syntax:

$obj1->myFun();

$obj2->myFun();

$obj3->myFun();

// Polymorphism refers to that multiple types of objects act on the same name function and obtain different results, which is called polymorphism.

e.g.

```php
<?php
class Work {
function complete(){}
}
class Task1 extends Work {
function complete() {
print "Task1 has been done.\n";
}}
class Task2 extends Work {
function complete() {
print "Task2 has been done.\n";
}}
class Task3 extends Work {
function complete() {
print "Task3 has been done.";
}}
$obj1=new Task1();  $obj1->complete();
$obj2=new Task2();  $obj2->complete();
$obj3=new Task3();  $obj3->complete();
?>
```

// Output:

Task1 has been done.

Task2 has been done.

Task3 has been done.

---

pow() syntax:

pow(m, n);
// Return m raised to the power of n.
e.g.
echo(**pow(2,3)**);   echo(**pow(-2,4)**);
// Output: 8   16

---

preg_match() syntax:
preg_match($pattern, $str);
// Check whether a match was found in a string.
// Return 1 if a match was found, return 0 if not.
e.g.
$str = "PowerShell in 8 Hours";
$pattern = "/shell/i";   // " i " means case insensitive
echo **preg_match($pattern, $str);**
// Output: 1

---

preg_match_all() syntax:
$match_number = preg_match_all($pattern, $string);
// Search for multiple matches in a string by regular expression.
// Return the number of matches in the string
// $pattern: regular expression indicating what to search for.
// $string: the string where the search will be performed.
e.g.
$str = "A cow plows field slowly in the downtown now";
$pattern = "/ow/i";   // find all occurrences of "**ow**" in a string
$match_num = **preg_match_all($pattern, $str);**
echo " The 'ow' occurrence number is $match_num";
// Output: The 'ow' occurrence number is 6

---

preg_replace() syntax:
preg_replace(str1, str2, $string)
// Use regular expression to replace the str1 with str2 in a string.
e.g.
$string = 'Scala in 8 Hours';

```
$pattern = '/scala/i';
echo preg_replace($pattern, 'Perl', $string);
// Output:   Perl in 8 Hours
```

---

preg_split() syntax:

preg_split($pattern, $string)

// Split a string to an array by using a pattern as separators

e.g.

```
$str = '10-12-2022';
$patt = '/\D/';     // Split anything which is not a digit
$array = preg_split($patt, $str);
print_r($array);
// Output:   Array([0] => 10   [1] => 12   [2] => 2022)
```

---

prepare() syntax:

prepare("insert into tablename(var1,var2,var3)values(?,?,?)")
prepare("select * from tablename where var1=? and var2=?")

// Prepare statement is used to execute multiple same SQL statements.

e.g.

```
<?php
$con=new mysqli("servername","username","password","db");
$stmt = $con->prepare("INSERT INTO myTable (firstname, lastname, email) VALUES (?, ?, ?)");
$stmt->bind_param("sss", $firstname, $lastname, $email); // bind
// "sss" means 3 strings. If "ids", it means 1 integer, 1 double, 1 string.
$firstname = "Ray";    $lastname = "Yao";
$email = "xxx@yyy.com";
$stmt->execute();    // run
echo "Insert data successfully";
?>
// Output:   Insert data successfully
```

---

prev() syntax:

prev($array)

// Return the previous element in the array

e.g.

$a = array("A ", "B ", "C ");

echo current($a); echo next($a); echo **prev($a)**;

// Output: A B A

---

print syntax:

print "content";

print ("content");

// Output string or value of a variable.

e.g.

print " Hello World! ";

print (" Hello World! ");

// Output: Hello World!   Hello World!

// The different between "echo" and "print":

// "echo" can output one or more strings, without return value.

// "print" only outputs one string and can return a value 1.

---

printf() syntax:

printf(" %format", $variable);

// Print a format string.

// Replace the %format with the value of $variable

// About %format, please see The String Format Chart.

e.g.

$num = 8; $str = "Hours";

printf("JAVA in %u %s.", $num, $str);

// $num replaces %u, $str replaces %s

// Output: JAVA in 8 Hours

---

print_r() syntax:

print_r($variable);

// Print or show information stored in a variable

e.g.

$var = array("A", "B", "C");

print_r($var);
// Output: Array ([0] => A   [1] => B   [2] => C)

---

private syntax:
private $variable=value;
private function $funName(){}

// The private variable and the private function are only accessed by the current class.

e.g.
```
<?php
class ParentClass{
```
private $a=30;   private $b=20;
```
function add() {
echo $this->a + $this->b." ";       // can access private variable
}}
class ChildClass extends ParentClass{
function sub(){
echo $this->a - $this->b." ";       // cannot access private variable
}}
$obj= new ChildClass;
$obj->add();
$obj->sub();
?>
```
// Output: 50   0
// PHP Warning: Undefined property: ChildClass::$a in line 9
// PHP Warning: Undefined property: ChildClass::$b in line 9

---

protected syntax:
protected $variable=value;
protected function $funName(){}

// The protected variable and the protected function are only accessed by the current class, the base class and the derived class.
// Without the relationship of base class and derived class, the protected member cannot be accessed.

e.g.
```php
<?php
class ParentClass{
protected $a=30;  protected $b=20;
function add() {
echo $this->a + $this->b." ";     // can access protected variable
}}
class ChildClass extends ParentClass{
function sub(){
echo $this->a - $this->b." ";     // can access protected variable
}}
$obj= new ChildClass;
$obj->add();
$obj->sub();
?>
// Output:    50    10
```

---

public syntax:

public $variable=value;
public function $funName(){}

// The public variable and the public function can be accessed by the current class, the base class and the derived class.

e.g.
```php
<?php
class ParentClass{
public $a=30;  public $b=20;
function add() {
echo $this->a + $this->b." ";     // can access public variable
}}
class ChildClass extends ParentClass{
function sub(){
echo $this->a - $this->b." ";     // can access public variable
}}
$obj= new ChildClass;
```

```php
$obj->add();
$obj->sub();
?>
```
// Output: 50   10

---

putenv() syntax:

putenv("VARIABLE=value");

// Set an environment variable and a value.

e.g.

putenv("USER=Ray Yao");

echo "The user name is: " . getenv("USER");

// Output: The user name is: Ray Yao

---

query() syntax:

connectVariable -> query(queryVariable)

// Execute the query

e.g.

```php
<?php
$con=new mysqli("servername","username","password","db");
  if(!$con->connect_errno){    // check connection
    $sql = "INSERT INTO myTable(name, age, email)
      VALUES (\"Ray Yao\", \"28\", \"xxx@yyy.com\")";
    if( $con->query($sql) ){    // $con->query($sql) runs query
      echo "Data inserted successfully.";
  }}
  $con->close();
?>
```
// Output: Data inserted successfully

---

radio button syntax:

<input type="radio" name="data" value="myValue">

// type="radio" is used to input data by single choice.

// name="data" specifies the inputted data that will be passed to the PHP file for processing.

// value="myValue" specifies one of the optional contents.

e.g.

```php
<?php
$data = isset($_GET['data'])? htmlentities($_GET['data']) : "";
if($data) {
     if($data =='Matlab') { echo 'Matlab in 8 Hours';}
     else if($data =='Kotlin') { echo 'Kotlin in 8 Hours'; }
     else if($data =='Pandas') { echo 'Pandas in 8 Hours'; }
} else {
?><form action="" method="get">
   <input type="radio" name="data" value="Matlab" />Matlab
   <input type="radio" name="data" value="Kotlin" />Kotlin
   <input type="radio" name="data" value="Pandas" />Pandas
   <input type="submit" value="Submit">
</form>
<?php
}
?>
```

// Output:

○ Matlab ⦿ Kotlin ○ Pandas [Submit]

Kotlin in 8 Hours

----

rand() syntax:

rand(min, max)

// Generate an integer from min to max

e.g.

echo(**rand**(100,1000));

// Output: 268

----

readfile() syntax:

readfile("filename", bool);

// Read a file. Set "bool" to true if search for the file in include_path.

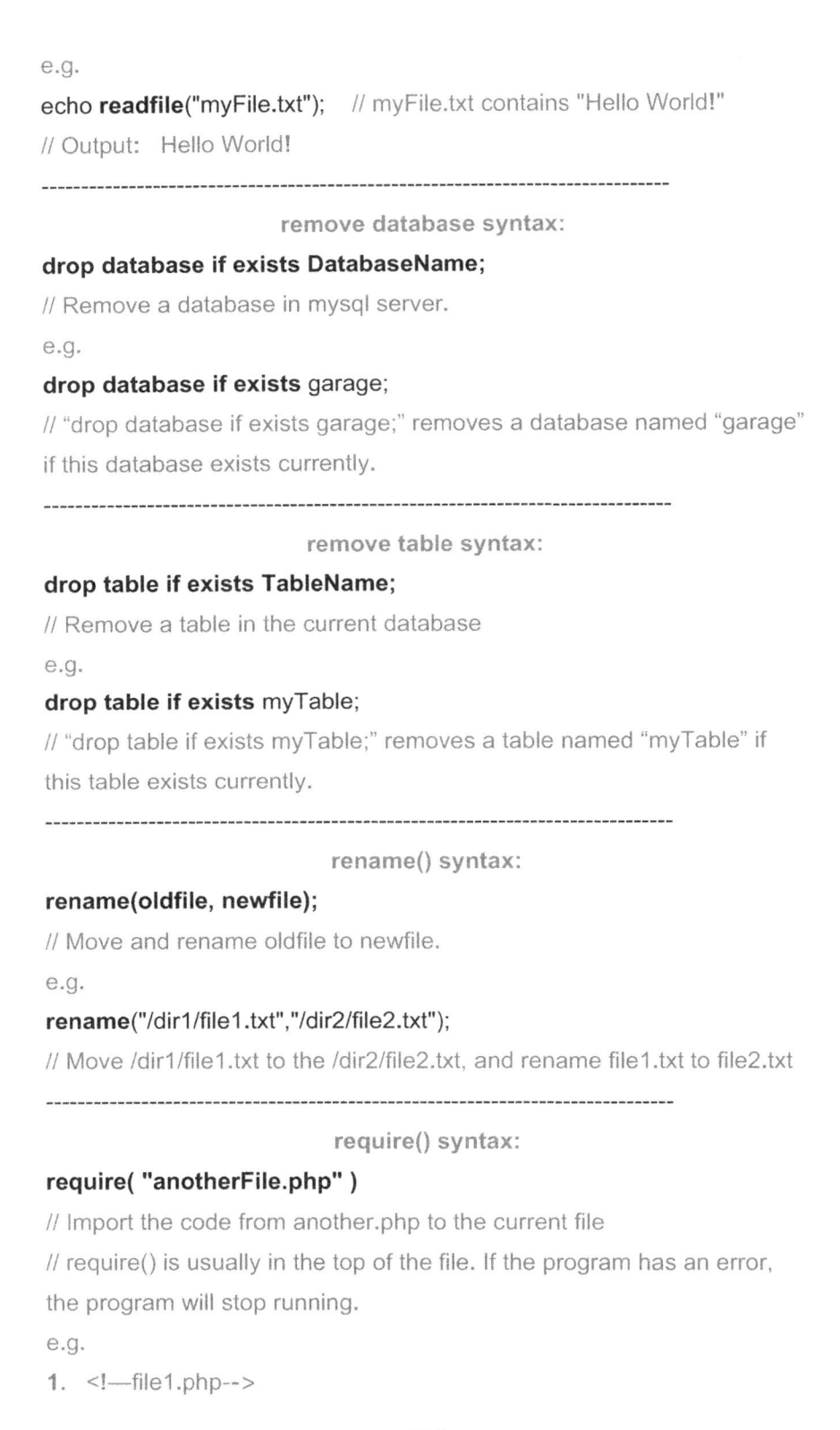

e.g.

echo **readfile**("myFile.txt");   // myFile.txt contains "Hello World!"

// Output: Hello World!

---

remove database syntax:

drop database if exists DatabaseName;

// Remove a database in mysql server.

e.g.

drop database if exists garage;

// "drop database if exists garage;" removes a database named "garage" if this database exists currently.

---

remove table syntax:

drop table if exists TableName;

// Remove a table in the current database

e.g.

drop table if exists myTable;

// "drop table if exists myTable;" removes a table named "myTable" if this table exists currently.

---

rename() syntax:

rename(oldfile, newfile);

// Move and rename oldfile to newfile.

e.g.

rename("/dir1/file1.txt","/dir2/file2.txt");

// Move /dir1/file1.txt to the /dir2/file2.txt, and rename file1.txt to file2.txt

---

require() syntax:

require("anotherFile.php")

// Import the code from another.php to the current file

// require() is usually in the top of the file. If the program has an error, the program will stop running.

e.g.

1.   <!—file1.php-->

```php
<?php  echo " From file1.php ";  ?>
```
2. <!--file2.php-->

```php
<?php
require("file1.php");   // import file1.php to here
echo " From file2.php ";
?>      <!--run file2.php-->
```
// Output: From file1.php   From file2.php

---

require_once() syntax:

require_once("anotherFile.php")

// Import the code from another.php to the current file for only once.

// require_once() is usually in the top of the file. If the program has an error, the program will stop running.

e.g.

1. <!--file1.php-->

```php
<?php  echo " From file1.php ";  ?>
```
2. <!--file2.php-->

```php
<?php
require_once("file1.php");   // import file1.php to here once
echo " From file2.php ";
?>
```
// Output: From file1.php   From file2.php

---

reset form syntax:

`<input type="reset"  value="xxx">`

// Reset all data in the form.

// "value" attribute sets the characters on the button.

e.g.

```html
<form action="myfile.php"  method="post">
<input type="reset"  value="RESET">
</form>
```
// Output:

    [RESET]

---

reset() syntax:

reset($array)

// Return the first element of an array.

e.g.

$arr = array("ant", "bee", "cat", "dog");

echo **reset($arr)**;

// Output: ant

---

return syntax:

return value;

// "return value" is used to return a value to the function caller.

e.g.

function multiply($x, $y){

return $x * $y;   // return the value to the function caller

}

echo(multiply(10,20));   // this is a function caller

// Output: 200

---

rmdir() syntax:

rmdir(/directory);

// Remove the empty directory.

e.g.

rmdir('/temp/mydir');   // mydir is an empty directory

// Remove the directory /temp/mydir

---

round() syntax:

round($float, decimal_places);

// Round up the $float according to the number of decimal places.

e.g.

var_dump(**round**(3.1415926535898, 3));

// Output: 3.142

---

rsort() syntax:

rsort($array)

// Sort the array element values in descending order

e.g.

$arr=array("30","10","20");

rsort($arr);   // sort element values

print_r($arr);

// Output: Array([0] => 30   [1] => 20   [2] => 10)

---

rtrim() syntax:

rtrim($string, $substring)

// Remove the spaces or substring from the right side of a string

e.g.

$str = "Hi, Friends";

echo **rtrim**($str, "Friends");   // remove Friends

// Output: Hi,

---

scandir() syntax:

scandir("/directory");

// Return all sub directories and files inside the specified directory.

e.g.

$array = **scandir**("/directory");

print_r($array);   // result vary

// Output: Array([0]=>. [1]=>.. [2]=>subDir [3]=>f1.php [4]=>f2.txt)

---

select data syntax:

SELECT columnName FROM tableName

SELECT * FROM tableName

// Select data from one or more tables. "*" means all columns

e.g.

<?php

$con=new mysqli("servername","username","password","db");

$sql = "SELECT id, firstname, lastname FROM myTable";

$result = $con->query($sql);   // execute the query

if ($result->num_rows > 0) {

while($row = $result->fetch_assoc()) {

```php
echo "ID: ". $row["id"]. " First Name: ". $row["firstname"]. "Last Name: ". $row["lastname"]. PHP_EOL;   // show data in each row
}} else {
  echo "0 results";
}
?>
```

// num_rows() returns how many rows of the table
// fetch_assoc() returns an assoc array that contains rows of a table. Its key is always a string type. For example: [string]=> value.

----

select data syntax:

$sql="select column from table-name";
$query=mysqli_query($con, $sql);

// $sql="select column from table-name" is used to retrieve table data by the column name from a table.
// $query=mysqli_query($con, $sql) executes the query.
// "$con" is the connection to MySql server. (See previous page).

e.g.

```php
<?php
$con= mysqli_connect( "localhost", "root", "12345678" );
if( $con ) {     // if connect MySQL server successfully
  echo " Connect successfully! ";
}
$select=mysqli_select_db( $con, "myDB" );
if( $select ) {   // if select database "myDB" successfully
  echo " Select myDB successfully!<br> ";
}   // assume that myDB has a table "colortable"
$sql="select id, color1 from colortable";
// select two columns "id" and "color1" in the table "colortable"
$query=mysqli_query( $con,$sql );   // run query
if( $query ) {
  echo " Retrieve data successfully! <br>";
}
while($row = mysqli_fetch_array($query)){   // return an array
```

```php
echo("<br> ID: ".$row["id"]);   // show $row["id"] value
echo("<br> color1: ".$row["color1"]);   // show $row["color1"] value
}
?>
```

// Output:

Connect successfully! Select myDB successfully!

Retrieve data successfully!

---

select to show table syntax:

select * from TableName;

// Show and view all data in a table of a database.

e.g.

use library;

select * from books;

```
+----+-------+-------+---------+
| id | title | price | author  |
+----+-------+-------+---------+
|  1 | Java  | 13.99 | Ray Yao |
|  2 | Html  | 12.88 | Ann Lee |
|  3 | Lamp  | 11.67 | Jan Poe |
+----+-------+-------+---------+
```

// "select * from books;" shows all data in the table "books".

// There are 3 records and 4 fields in the table "books" of the "library".

---

select option syntax:

<select name="data", id="xx" multiple size = number>

  <option value="">Please select one item</option>

  <option value="value1">text1</option>

  <option value="value2">text2</option>

  <option value="value3">text3</option>

</select>

// Get the value of the drop-down menu by the name property of the select. If it is multiple selection, please use "multiple size='number'".

e.g.

```php
<?php
$data = isset($_GET['data'])? htmlentities($_GET['data']) : "";
```

```php
if($data) {    // get the data value from the form
     if($data =='MATLAB') { echo 'Matlab in 8 Hours'; }
     else if($data =='KOTLIN') { echo 'Kotlin in 8 Hours'; }
     else if($data =='PANDAS') { echo 'Pandas in 8 Hours'; }
} else {
?>
<form action="" method="get">
  <select name="data">
    <option value="">Please select one book</option>
    <option value="MATLAB">Matlab</option>
    <option value="KOTLIN">Kotlin</option>
    <option value="PANDAS">Pandas</option>
  </select>
<input type="submit" value="Submit">
</form>
<?php
}
?>
// Output:
```

Kotlin ⌄   Submit

Kotlin in 8 Hours

----

serialize() syntax:

serialize(values);

// Create a storable representation of values.

e.g.

```php
$var = serialize(array("ant", "bee", "cat", "dog"));
echo $var;
// Output:  a:4:{i:0;s:3:"ant";i:1;s:3:"bee";i:2;s:3:"cat";i:3;s:3:"dog";}
```

----

session_destroy() syntax:

session_destroy();

// Destroy all of the data related to the current session.

e.g.

session_start();

$_SESSION["color"]="red";

session_destroy();

echo "Session has been destroyed ";

// Output: Session has been destroyed

---

session_id()syntax:

<?php session_start()?>   // start a session

<a href = "anotherPage.php<?php echo(SID);?>">...</a>

// pass the session id to another page

<?php echo(session_id());?>   // show session id

e.g.

1.   <!-- aFile.php -->

<?php session_start()?>   <!-- start php session -->

\
Here is "First Page".\

\
Send out a session id to the second page\
\

<a href = "bFile.php<?php echo(SID);?>">To Second Page</a>

<!-- pass session id to the bFile.php -->

<!-- save this file with the name "aFile.php" in the working folder-->

2.   <!-- bFile.php -->

<?php session_start()?>   <!-- start php session -->

\
Here is "Second Page".\

\
The session id is: \
\

<?php echo(session_id());?>   <!-- show session id -->

<!-- save the file with the name "bFile.php" in the working folder-->

<!-- please run the aFile.php -->

// Output:

Here is "First Page".

Send out a session id to the second page

<u>To Second Page</u>

// Output:

Here is "Second Page".

The session id is:

m4tiga6576moc23dma5jugt8cm

---

session_name() syntax:

session_name("name")   // set a session name

session_name()   // get the session name

e.g.

session_name('mySession');   // set a session name

session_start();

echo **session_name**();   // get the session name

// Output: mySession

---

session_regenerate_id() syntax:

session_regenerate_id();

// Create a new session id, without losing any current session information except the session id.

e.g.

session_start();

echo session_id()."\n";

session_regenerate_id();

echo session_id();

// Output: a5d7850ff6afa6135b17e6dd69ec0a22
           b6p9861rf8bib7057a32v8ap36gd7b68

---

session_start() syntax:

<?php session_start()?>   // start a session

<a href = "anotherPage.php<?php echo(SID);?>">...</a>

// pass the session id to another page

<?php echo(session_id());?>   // show session id

e.g.

1. <!-- aFile.php -->

<?php session_start()?>   <!-- start php session -->

Here is "First Page".

\<br\>Send out a session id to the second page\<br\>\<br\>

\<a href = "bFile.php\<?php echo(SID);?\>"\>To Second Page\</a\>

\<!-- pass session id to the bFile.php --\>

\<!-- save this file with the name "aFile.php" in the working folder--\>

2.   \<!-- bFile.php --\>

\<?php session_start()?\>   \<!-- start php session --\>

\<br\>Here is "Second Page".\<br\>

\<br\>The session id is: \<br\>\<br\>

\<?php echo(session_id());?\>   \<!-- show session id --\>

\<!-- save the file with the name "bFile.php" in the working folder--\>

\<!-- please run the aFile.php --\>

// Output:

Here is "First Page".

Send out a session id to the second page

To Second Page

// Output:

Here is "Second Page".

The session id is:

m4tiga6576moc23dma5jugt8cm

---

session_status() syntax:

session_status()   // Return the session status 0, 1, 2

0 – PHP_SESSION_DISABLED: Sessions are currently disabled.

1 – PHP_SESSION_NONE: No session has been started.

2 – PHP_SESSION_ACTIVE: A session has been started.

e.g.

session_start();

$sta = **session_status();**

echo ("Current session status is: ".$sta);

// Output: Current session status is: 2

---

session_unset() syntax:

session_unset();

// Release all session variables

e.g.

session_start();

$_SESSION['flower'] = 'Rose';

echo $_SESSION['flower'];

session_unset();

echo $_SESSION['flower'];   // session variable has been released

// Output: Rose

// PHP Warning: Undefined array key "flower" on line 6

----

session_write_close() syntax:

session_write_close();

// Save the session data and end the current session.

e.g.

session_start();

session_write_close();

// Output: Returns true if succeeds, return false if fails

----

set_error_handler() syntax:

set_error_handler("myErrorHandler")

// Set a user-defined error handler

"myErrorHandler(myHandler($errno, $errmsg, $errfile, $errline){...}

// A user-defined function for handling the error.

e.g.

<?php

function myHandler($errno, $errmsg, $errfile, $errline){

echo " Error No:[$errno]. Error Message:$errmsg. ";

echo " Error Line:$errline. Error File:$errfile. ";

}

set_error_handler("myHandler");   // user-defined error handler

$var = -100;

if ($var<0) { trigger_error("A custom error triggered");}

?>

// Output:

Error No:[1024]. Error Message:A custom error triggered. Error Line:8. Error File:/server/script.php.

---

set_exception_handler() syntax:

set_exception_handler("handlerFunction");
// Set a user-defined exception handler function.
e.g.
```
<?php
function myHandler($e){    // handler function
echo $e->getMessage();
}
set_exception_handler("myHandler");
throw new Exception("An exception occurs!");
?>
```
// Output: An exception occurs!

---

setcookie() syntax:

setcookie("name", "value");   // set cookie name and value
$_COOKIE["name"]; // get cookie value by cookie name
e.g.
1. // in aFile.php
```
<?php
setcookie("color", "blue");   // set a cookie
// cookie name is "color", cookie value is "blue"
header("location: bFile.php");      // redirect to bFile.php
?>
```
<!--save this file with the name "aFile.php" in the working folder-->

2. // in bFile.php
```
<?php
$mycolor = $_COOKIE["color"];  // get the cookie from aFile.php
// get the cookie whose name is "color"
echo $mycolor;    // show the color's value
?>
```
<!--save the file with the name "bFile.php" in the working folder-->

```
<!--please run the aFile.php-->
```
// Output: blue

---

sha1() syntax:

sha1(string)

// Perform a sha1 hash encryption on a string.

e.g.

echo **sha1**("Hello");

// Output: f7ff9e8b7bb2e09b70935a5d785e0cc5d9d0abf0

---

sha1_file() syntax:

sha1_file(file)

// Perform a sha1 hash encryption on a file.

e.g.

echo **sha1_file**("myFile.txt");

// Output: acg1r62dpcv8s9h5brwus0cq23kdz67g92b3gsb8

---

show databases syntax:

show databases;

// View all the available databases in the current mysql server.

e.g.

mysql > show databases;

```
+--------------------+
| Database           |
+--------------------+
| information_schema |
| mysql              |
| performance_schema |
| sakila             |
| sys                |
| world              |
+--------------------+
6 rows in set (0.00 sec)
```

---

show specified field syntax:

select field1, field2, field3 from TableName;

// show some specified fields in a table

e.g.

\# 1. Given the current status of the table "books" as follows:

use library;

select * **from** books;

```
+----+-------+----------+-------+-------+---------+
| id | title | writer   | pages | price | publish |
+----+-------+----------+-------+-------+---------+
|  1 | Java  | Ray Yao  |  200  | 13.99 |  2018   |
|  2 | Ajax  | Ann Lee  |  190  | 12.88 |  2019   |
|  4 | Ruby  | Ray Yao  |  200  | 13.99 |  2017   |
|  5 | Rust  | R.Y.     |  128  | 12.99 |  2016   |
|  6 | Node  | R.Y.     |  128  | 12.99 |  2020   |
+----+-------+----------+-------+-------+---------+
```

\# 2. Show some specified fields

use library;

select title, price **from** books;

```
+-------+-------+
| title | price |
+-------+-------+
| Java  | 13.99 |
| Ajax  | 12.88 |
| Ruby  | 13.99 |
| Rust  | 12.99 |
| Node  | 12.99 |
+-------+-------+
```

// "select title, price from books;" only shows two fields "title, price" in the table "books".

---

show specified record syntax:

select * **from** TableName where field = value;

// Show a specified record in a table.

e.g.

\# 1. Given the current status of the table "books" as follows:

use library;

select * **from** books;

```
+----+-------+----------+-------+-------+---------+
| id | title | writer   | pages | price | publish |
+----+-------+----------+-------+-------+---------+
|  1 | Java  | Ray Yao  |  200  | 13.99 |  2018   |
|  2 | Ajax  | Ann Lee  |  190  | 12.88 |  2019   |
|  4 | Ruby  | Ray Yao  |  200  | 13.99 |  2017   |
|  5 | Rust  | R.Y.     |  128  | 12.99 |  2016   |
|  6 | Node  | R.Y.     |  128  | 12.99 |  2020   |
+----+-------+----------+-------+-------+---------+
```

2. Add a record, and then show this record

use library;

insert into books (id, title, writer, pages, price, publish)

values (7, "Lamp", "Jan Poe",120, 11.67, 2015);

select * **from** books **where** writer = "Jan Poe";

```
+----+-------+---------+-------+-------+---------+
| id | title | writer  | pages | price | publish |
+----+-------+---------+-------+-------+---------+
|  7 | Lamp  | Jan Poe |   120 | 11.67 |    2015 |
+----+-------+---------+-------+-------+---------+
```

// "select * from books where writer = "Jan Poe";" only shows the record where writer is Jan Poe.

---

show tables syntax:

show tables;

// Show all existing tables in the current database.

e.g.

mysql> use world;

Database changed

mysql> show tables;

```
+-----------------+
| Tables_in_world |
+-----------------+
| city            |
| country         |
| countrylanguage |
+-----------------+
```

// "use world;" specifies to use a database "world".

// "show tables" displays all tables in the database "world".

// There are three tables totally in the database "world".

---

shuffle() syntax:

shuffle($array)

// Shuffle the order of array elements at random.

e.g.

$arr = array("a", "b", "c", "d");

shuffle($arr);

print_r($arr);

// Output: Array([0] => c   [1] => b   [2] => d   [3] => a)

---

simplexml_load_file() syntax:
$xml = simplexml_load_file("myFile.xml")
$xml -> node

// Get data from a xml file, and print out contents according to nodes

e.g.

1. Assume that the content of myFile.xml is:

```
<?xml version='1.0' encoding='UTF-8'?>
 <note>
   <from>Ray Yao</from>
   <greeting>Hi, My friend!</greeting>
 </note>
```

2.

```
<?php
$xml=simplexml_load_file("myFile.xml") or die("Error!");
echo $xml->from."<br>";
echo $xml->greeting."<br>";
?>
```

// Output: Ray Yao   Hi, My friend!

---

simplexml_load_string() syntax:
simplexml_load_string(myXmlData)

// Get XML data of a string and print them out.

e.g.

```
<?php
$myXML="<?xml version='1.0' encoding='UTF-8'?>
<note>
<from>Ray Yao</from>
<greeting>Hi, My friend!</greeting>
</note>";
$xml=simplexml_load_string($myXML) or die("Error!");
print_r($xml);
?>
```

// Output:

SimpleXMLElement Object(

   [from] => Ray Yao

   [greeting] => Hi, My friend!

)

---

sleep() syntax:

sleep(seconds)

// Delay running the current code for a specified seconds

e.g.

sleep(3);

// Pause for 3 seconds before continuing.

---

sort() syntax:

sort($array)

// Sort the array element values in ascending order

e.g.

$arr=array("30","10","20");

sort($arr);   // sort element values

print_r($arr);

// Output: Array([0] => 10   [1] => 20   [2] => 30)

---

sort table data syntax:

order by field asc / desc;

// Sort data in ascending order by using "asc" keyword.

// Sort data in descending order by using "desc" keyword.

e.g.

1. Given the current status of the table "books" as follows:

use library;

select * from books;

```
+----+-------+---------+-------+-------+---------+
| id | title | writer  | pages | price | publish |
+----+-------+---------+-------+-------+---------+
|  1 | Java  | Ray Yao |  200  | 13.99 |  2018   |
|  2 | Ajax  | Ann Lee |  190  | 12.88 |  2019   |
|  3 | Html  | Jan Poe |  110  | 10.99 |  2014   |
|  4 | Ruby  | Ray Yao |  200  | 13.99 |  2017   |
|  5 | Rust  | R.Y.    |  128  | 12.99 |  2016   |
|  6 | Node  | R.Y.    |  128  | 12.99 |  2020   |
|  7 | Lamp  | Jan Poe |  120  | 11.67 |  2015   |
+----+-------+---------+-------+-------+---------+
```

2. Sort the table by using "asc"

use library;

select * from books **order by** price **asc**;

```
+----+-------+---------+-------+-------+---------+
| id | title | writer  | pages | price | publish |
+----+-------+---------+-------+-------+---------+
|  3 | Html  | Jan Poe |  110  | 10.99 |  2014   |
|  7 | Lamp  | Jan Poe |  120  | 11.67 |  2015   |
|  2 | Ajax  | Ann Lee |  190  | 12.88 |  2019   |
|  5 | Rust  | R.Y.    |  128  | 12.99 |  2016   |
|  6 | Node  | R.Y.    |  128  | 12.99 |  2020   |
|  1 | Java  | Ray Yao |  200  | 13.99 |  2018   |
|  4 | Ruby  | Ray Yao |  200  | 13.99 |  2017   |
+----+-------+---------+-------+-------+---------+
```

// "select * from books order by price asc;" sorts the "price" data in ascending order.

---

sprintf() syntax:

$variable = sprintf("%format", $variable);

// Write a formatted string to a new variable

// Replace the %format with the value of $variable

// About %format, please see The String Format Chart.

e.g.

$num = 8; $str = "Hours";

$var = sprintf("JAVA in %u %s.", $num, $str);

// $num replaces %u, $str replaces %s

echo $var;

// Output: JAVA in 8 Hours

---

sqrt() syntax:

sqrt(number):

// Return a square root of a number

e.g.

echo(**sqrt**(25).' ');   echo(**sqrt**(0.81).' ');

// Output: 5   0.9

---

sscanf() syntax:

sscanf($string, "%format");

// Parse a string according to the specified format.

// About %format, please see The String Format Chart.

e.g.

$str = "Java in 8 Hours";

$format = **sscanf($str,"%s %s %d %s");**

print_r($format);

// Output: Array([0] => Java   [1] => in   [2] => 8   [3] => Hours)

---

static syntax:

static $variable = value;

// Static variable can retain the value from the last time the function was called.

e.g.

```
<?php function myFun() {
static $var=10;
echo $var++;   // $var value will keep to next function call
echo " ";
}
myFun();  myFun();  myFun();
?>
```

// Output: 10 11 12

---

static member syntax:

static $variable = value;

static function funName(){...}

ClassName::$variable   // the class references the variable

ClassName::funName()   // the class references the function

// The static member can be directly called by a class, not by an object.

e.g.

```php
<?php
class MyClass {
public static $staticVar = 'I am a static variable';
public static function staticFun(){
    echo "I am a static function";
}}
print MyClass::$staticVar . PHP_EOL;   // called by a class
print MyClass::staticFun() . PHP_EOL;   // called by a class
?>
```

// Output:

I am a static variable

I am a static function

----

string syntax:

$str = "characters";

$str = 'characters';

// String consist of a sires of characters, which are enclosed by double quotes or single quotes usually.

e.g.

$x = " Hello world! ";

echo $x;

$y = ' Hi, my friend! ';

echo $y;

// Output: Hello world!   Hi, my friend!

----

string connecting syntax:

$string1 . " " . $string2

// Connect two strings

e.g.

$book1 = "PowerShell";

$book2 = "in 8 Hours";

echo **$book1 . " " . $book2**;

// Output: PowerShell in 8 Hours

---

stripos() syntax:

stripos(string, substring)

// Return the position of the first occurrence of the substring in string.

// stripos() is case insensitive.

e.g.

echo **stripos**("Powershell & Shell Scripting in 8 Hours", "Shell");

// Output: 5

---

stripslashes() syntax:

stripslashes("backslashes")

// Remove backslashes \ and \\.

e.g.

echo **stripslashes**("I don\'t know!");

// Output: I don't know!

---

stristr() syntax:

stristr("string", "substring")

// Search for the first occurrence of a substring and return the rest part.

e.g.

echo **stristr**("Hi, My friends!", "my");   // stristr() is case insensitive

// Output: My Friends!

---

strip_tags() syntax:

strip_tags("string_with_html_tags");

// Remove any html tags from a string.

e.g.

echo **strip_tags**("The book is 'R in 8 Hours'");

// Output: The book is 'R in 8 Hours'

---

str_ireplace() syntax:

str_ireplace(old_str, "new_str", "original_str")

// In the original string, replace a old string with a new string.

e.g.

// str_ireplace() is case insensitive
echo **str_ireplace**("JQuery", "MySQL", "jQuery in 8 Hours");
// Output: MySQL in 8 Hours

---

strlen( ) syntax:
strlen($string);
// Return a length of a string and space
e.g.
$string=" Hello World! ";
echo **strlen($string);**   // return string length
// Output: 16

---

str_pad() syntax:
str_pad(string, length, pad)
// Pad a string to a specified length
e.g.
$str = "So Good";
echo **str_pad**($str,10,"$");   // pad by "$" to the length as 10
// Output: So Good$$$

---

strpbrk() syntax:
strpbrk("string", "character")
// Search a string for the specified character that is the first occurrence and return the rest substring.
e.g.
echo **strpbrk**("NumPy in 8 Hours", "i");   // strpbrk() is case sensitive
// Output: in 8 Hours

---

strpos() syntax:
strpos(string, substring)
// Return the position of the first occurrence of the substring in string.
// strpos() is case sensitive.
e.g.
echo **strpos**("Powershell & Shell Scripting in 8 Hours", "Shell");

// Output: 13

---

str_repeat() syntax:

str_repeat(string, repeat_number)

// Repeat a string according to the specified number of times

e.g.

echo **str_repeat**("Good! ", 3);   // repeat 3 times

// Output: Good! Good! Good!

---

strrev() syntax:

strrev("string")

// Reverse a string

e.g.

echo **strrev**("abcde");

// Output: edcba

---

strripos() syntax:

strripos(string, substring)

// Return the position of the last occurrence of the substring in string.

// strripos() is case insensitive.

e.g.

echo **strripos**("Powershell & Shell Scripting in 8 Hours", "shell");

// Output: 13

---

strrpos() syntax:

strrpos(string, substring)

// Return the position of the last occurrence of the substring in string.

// strrpos() is case sensitive.

e.g.

echo **strrpos**("Powershell & Shell Scripting in 8 Hours", "shell");

// Output: 5

---

strstr() syntax:

strstr("string", "substring")

// Search for the first occurrence of a substring and return the rest part.
e.g.
echo **strstr**("Hi, My friends!", "My");   // strstr() is case sensitive
// Output: My Friends!

---

strtolower( ) syntax:

strtolower($string);

// Return a lowercase string

e.g.

$string=" Hello World! ";

echo **strtolower($string);**   // return lowercase

// Output: hello world!

---

strtotime() syntax:

strtotime()

// Return the number of seconds since January 1 1970 00:00:00 GMT

e.g.

echo(**strtotime**("now")." ");

echo(**strtotime**("next Friday")." ");

echo(**strtotime**("last Monday")." ");

// Output: 1667875862   1668124800   1667779200

---

strtoupper() syntax:

strtoupper($string);

// Return a uppercase string

e.g.

$string=" Hello World! ";

echo **strtoupper($string);**   // return uppercase

// Output: HELLO WORLD!

---

str_replace() syntax:

str_replace(old_str, "new_str", "original_str")

// In the original string, replace a old string with a new string.

e.g.

// str_replace() is case sensitive

echo **str_replace**("Rust", "Perl", "Rust in 8 Hours");

// Output: Perl in 8 Hours

---

str_shuffle() syntax:

str_shuffle("string")

// Shuffle all characters of a string at random.

e.g.

echo **str_shuffle**("abcde");

// Output: bdaec

---

str_split() syntax:

str_split("string")

// Split a string to an array

e.g.

print_r(**str_split**("html"));

// Output: Array([0] => h   [1] => t   [2] => m   [3] => l)

---

str_word_count() syntax:

str_word_count("string")

// Count the words in a string. (except count the digit.)

e.g.

echo **str_word_count**("Hi, My friends!");   // 3 words

// Output: 3

---

strtr() syntax:

$array = array(key=>value);   // the value will replace the key

strtr("string", $array);   // all values of array replace the string

// Replace the string with an array values

e.g.

$arr = array("Hi," => "Hello,", "Friends" => "World");

echo **strtr("Hi, Friends", $arr)**; // "Hello, World" replaces "Hi, Friends"

// Output: Hello, World

---

submit form syntax:

<input type="submit" value="xxx">

// Submit all data in the form to the server.

// "value" attribute sets the characters on the button.

e.g.

<form action="myfile.php" method="post">

<input type="submit" value="SUBMIT">

</form>

// Output:

```
| SUBMIT |
```

---

substr() syntax:

substr(string, start, length)

// Extract a substring by the specified parameters

// "start" specifies the index where to start to extract

// "length" specified the length to extract

e.g.

echo **substr("JavaScript in 8 Hours!",4,6)**;

// Output: Script

---

substr_count() syntax:

substr_count("string", "word")

// Count how many the specified word occurs in a string.

e.g.

echo **substr_count**("OK! It is OK!", "OK");   // count "OK"

// Output: 2

---

substr_replace() syntax:

substr_replace(string, new, start)

// Replace part of string with new string from the specified position

// "start" specified a position where the replacement occurs.

e.g.

echo **substr_replace**("12345678", "OK", 3);

// Output: 123OK

---

switch syntax:

switch ($variable) {

case 1: // if equals this case, do this; **break;**

case 2: // if equals this case, do this; **break;**

case 3: // if equals this case, do this; **break;**

default : // if not equals any case, run default code; **break;**

}

// $variable value will compare each case first, if it equals one of the "case" value; it will run that "case" code. Otherwise, run default code.

e.g.

$number=20;

switch ($number) {   // $number will compare each case

case 10 : echo "Running case 10"; break;

case 20 : echo "Running case 20"; break;   // match

case 30 : echo "Running case 30"; break;

default : echo "Running default code"; break; }

// Output: Running case 20

---

text input syntax:

<input type="text" name="data">

// input type="text" specifies the input type is "text",

// name="data" specifies the inputted "data" that will be passed to the PHP file for processing.

e.g.

<html>

<form action=" " method="post">

Name: **<input type="text" name="myName">**

<input type="submit" value="Submit">

</form>

<?php echo $_POST["myName"]; ?>

</html>

// Output:

Name: Ray Yao   Submit

Ray Yao

---

textarea input syntax:
<textarea name="xxx" rows="num" cols="num">

// "textarea" type is used to input data in a text area.
// "rows" specifics the number of rows.
// "cols" specifics the number of columns.

e.g.

```
<html>
<form action="" method="POST">
 <textarea name="book" rows="3" cols="20"></textarea>
 <p><input type="submit" value="Submit"></p>
</form>
</html>
<?php
 $book = $_POST['book'];
 echo "$book";
?>
```

// Output:

```
Scala in 8 Hours
```

Submit

Scala in 8 Hours

---

time() syntax:
time()

// Return the current Unix timestamp (seconds) since the Unix Epoch (from January 1st, 1970, 00:00:00 GMT to now)

e.g.

var_dump(time());

// Output: int(1669305569)

---

trait syntax:

<?php trait TraitName{...} ?>   // declare a trait

<?php class MyClass{ use TraitName; } ?>   // use the trait

// Trait is used to define a method that can be used in multiple classes.

// Trait enables programmers to reuse a method in different classes.

e.g.

```php
<?php
trait myTrait {   // declare a trait
  public function myFun() {
    echo "This is a trait sample";
}}
class MyClass {
  use myTrait;   // use the trait
}
$obj = new MyClass();
$obj->myFun();
?>
```

// Output: This is a trait sample

---

trigger_error() syntax:

trigger_error("message")

// Triggered by an error and show an error message.

e.g.

```php
$var = -100;
if($var<0){trigger_error("Variable value must > 0 ");}
```

// Output:

Notice: Variable value must > 0 in /server/script.php on line 3.

---

trim() syntax:

trim($str, "characters");   // remove string characters in both sides

trim($str);   // remove string whitespaces in both sides

e.g.

$str1 = "ABC 123"; $str2 = "   Hi, My friends!   ";

echo **trim($str1,"A3")." ";**   // remove A and 3

echo **trim($str2);**   // remove spaces in both sides

Output: BC 12   Hi, My friends!

---

try / throw / catch() syntax:

try{...}   // contain some codes may cause exception

throw new Exception("message");   // throw an exception

catch{...}   // catch and handle the exception

e.g.

```
<?php
function myFun($num){
if($num<0){
```
throw new Exception("The variable value must be greater than 1");

}   // throw an exception

return true;

}

try{

myFun(-100);   // call the function

echo 'No this text is output if an exception has been thrown';

}

catch(Exception $e){   // catch the exception

echo $e->getMessage();   // show the exception message

}

?>

// Output: The variable value must be greater than 1

---

ucfirst() syntax:

ucfirst("string")

// Covert the first character of the string to uppercase.

e.g.

echo **ucfirst**("jQuery in 8 Hours");

// Output: JQuery in 8 Hours

---

ucwords() syntax:

ucwords("string")

// Convert the first character of each word in a string to uppercase.

e.g.

echo **ucwords**("c# cheat sheet");

// Output: C# Cheat Sheet

---

uniqid() syntax:

uniqid();

// Return a unique ID according to the current time in microseconds

e.g.

echo **uniqid();**

// Output: 637fc503919e3

---

unlink() syntax:

unlink("filename");

// Delete a file

e.g.

unlink("myFile.txt");

// Remove the "myFile.txt"

---

unserialize() syntax:

unserialize($serialized_data)

// Convert serialized data back to original value.

e.g.

$var = serialize(array("ant", "bee", "cat", "dog"));

echo $var;

$arr = **unserialize($var);**

print_r($arr);

// Output: a:4:{i:0;s:3:"ant";i:1;s:3:"bee";i:2;s:3:"cat";i:3;s:3:"dog";}
              Array([0] => ant   [1] => bee   [2] => cat   [3] => dog)

---

unset() syntax:

unset($variable)

// Remove the value of the $variable

e.g.

$str = "Hi, My friend!";

unset($str);

echo "After unset, the 'str' value is: " . $str;

// Output: After unset, the 'str' value is:

----

update table syntax:

$sql="update table-name set column-name=value where id=int";

$query=mysqli_query($con, $sql);

// "update table-name set column-name=value where id=int" can update a value in a specified column of the table.

// $query=mysqli_query($con, $sql) executes the query.

// "$con" is the connection to MySql server. (See mysqli_connect()).

e.g.

```
<?php
$con= mysqli_connect( "localhost", "root", "12345678" );
if( $con ) {    // if connect MySQL server successfully
echo  " Connect successfully! ";
}
$select=mysqli_select_db( $con, "myDB" );
if( $select ) {   // if select database "myDB" successfully
echo  " Select myDB successfully!<br> ";
}    // assume that myDB has a table "colortable"
$sql="update colortable set color5='sky' where id =1 ";
// set "sky" value to color5 column where id is 1
$query=mysqli_query( $con, $sql);   // run query
if( $query ) {
echo  " Update successfully! ";
}
?>
```

// Output:

Connect successfully! Select myDB successfully!

Update successfully!

----

update table syntax:

update TableName **set** field1 = value1, field2 = value2
where field = value;

// Update fields' values of a table in a database.

// "where field = value" can select a record to update fields.

e.g.

\# 1. Given the current status of the table "books" as follows:

use library;

select * **from** books;

```
+----+-------+---------+-------+-------+---------+
| id | title | writer  | pages | price | publish |
+----+-------+---------+-------+-------+---------+
|  1 | Java  | Ray Yao |     0 |  0.00 |    0000 |
|  2 | Ajax  | Ann Lee |     0 |  0.00 |    0000 |
+----+-------+---------+-------+-------+---------+
```

\# 2. Update the values of the specified fields:

update books **set** pages = 200, price = 13.99, publish = 2018
where title = "Java";

update books **set** pages = 190, price = 12.88, publish = 2019
where title = "Ajax";

select * **from** books;

```
+----+-------+---------+-------+-------+---------+
| id | title | writer  | pages | price | publish |
+----+-------+---------+-------+-------+---------+
|  1 | Java  | Ray Yao |   200 | 13.99 |    2018 |
|  2 | Ajax  | Ann Lee |   190 | 12.88 |    2019 |
+----+-------+---------+-------+-------+---------+
```

// "where title = "Java";" selects a record whose title is "Java" to update three fields (pages, price, publish).

// "where title = "Ajax";" selects a record whose title is "Ajax" to update three fields (pages, price, publish).

---

urldecode() syntax:

urldecode("encoded_data")

// Decode the encoded data back to the original data.

e.g.

$encode_data = urlencode("https://www.amazon.com/");
echo $encode_data."\n";

$decode_data = **urldecode($encode_data);**

echo $decode_data;

// Output: https%3A%2F%2Fwww.amazon.com%2F
          https://www.amazon.com/

---

urlencode() syntax:

urlencode("data")

// Encode the specified data.

e.g.

echo **urlencode**("https://www.amazon.com/");

// Output: https%3A%2F%2Fwww.amazon.com%2F

Use Database syntax:

use DatabaseName;

// Select a database in mysql server.

e.g.

mysql> use myDatabase;

Database changed

// "use myDatabase;" specifies to use a database named "myDatabase".

// "Database changed" is responding message from the server.

---

usleep() syntax:

usleep(microseconds)

// Delay running the current code for a specified microseconds

e.g.

usleep(3000000);

// Pause for 3000000 microsecond before continuing.

---

variable syntax:

$variable = value;

// variable name starts with "$" symbol.

e.g.

$var = 100;   // define a variable

$abcde = "Hello World";   // define a variable

$my_variable = "Number1";   // define a variable

echo ("$var $abcde $my_variable");

// Output: 100 Hello World Number1

---

var_dump() syntax:

var_dump($var);

// Return the type and value of a variable

e.g.

$x = 100;   **var_dump($x);**

$y = 3.14;   **var_dump($y);**

// Output: int(100)   float(3.14)

---

where condition syntax:

SELECT columnName FROM tableName WHERE columnName operator value

// Extract only those records that meet with the specified condition

e.g.

$sql = "SELECT id, firstname, lastname FROM myTable **WHERE id='1001'**";

// Return the record where id is 1001

---

while Loop syntax:

while (test-expression) {   // some php codes in here; **}**

// Loop through a block of code if the specified condition is true.

e.g.

$counter=0;

while ($counter < 8){   // loop at most 8 times

echo "&";

$counter++;   // increase 1 every loop

}

// Output: &&&&&&&&

---

wordwrap() syntax:

wordwrap($string, length, "\n");

// Wrap a string to a new line when it reaches a specific length.
e.g.
$str = "'Google Sheet in 8 Hours' is a very good book.";
echo **wordwrap($str,18,"\n")**;   // at most 18 characters each line
// Output:
'Google Sheet in 8
Hours' is a very
good book.

---

xml dom parser syntax:

$xmlObj = new DOMDocument();   // create a dom document object
$xmlObj->load("myFile.xml");   // load a xml file
print $xmlObj->saveXML();   // print out the contents of an xml file
// Get data from an xml file, and print out contents according to nodes.
e.g.
1. Assume that the content of myFile.xml is:
<?xml version='1.0' encoding='UTF-8'?>
<note>
<from>Ray Yao</from>
<greeting>Hi, My friend!</greeting>
</note>
2.
<?php
$obj = **new DOMDocument()**;
$obj->**load("myFile.xml")**;
print $obj->**saveXML()**;
?>
// Output: Ray Yao   Hi, My friend!

Appendix

PHP Reserved Words Chart

and	array( )	break
case	const	continue
default	do	echo( )
else	else if	empty( )
eval( )	exception	exit( )
extends	false	for
function	foreach	global
if	include( )	include_once( )
isset( )	list( )	new
null	or	print( )
require( )	require_once( )	return( )
static	switch	true
unset( )	xor	while

PHP Escaping Characters Chart

\n	outputs content to the next new line.
\r	makes a return
\t	makes a tab
\'	outputs a single quotation mark.
\"	outputs a double quotation mark.

PHP Predefined Characters Chart

Predefined Chars	Becomes
& (ampersand)	&amp;
" (double quote)	&quot;
' (single quote)	&#039;
< (less than)	&lt;
> (greater than)	&gt;

PHP File Opening Mode Chart

Mode	Operation
r	open file for reading only, from the beginning.
r+	open file for reading & writing, from the beginning.
w	open file for writing only, clear original content.
w+	open file for writing & reading, clear original content.
a	open file for writing only, append new content.
a+	open file for reading & writing, append new content.
x	create a new file for writing only.
x+	create a new file for reading & writing.

PHP Email Functions Chart

mail(to,subject,message,headers,parameters)

Arguments	Descriptions
to	The receiver / receivers of the email
subject	The subject of the email
message	The message to be sent, limit 70 chars per line
headers	The headers, such as From, Cc, and Bcc
parameters	The additional parameter of the email program

PHP Filter Functions Chart

Function	Description
filter_has_var()	checks whether a variable of a specified input exist
filter_id()	returns the filter id of a specified filter name
filter_input()	gets a value from form input and optionally filters it
filter_input_array()	gets values from form input and optionally filters them
filter_list()	returns a list of all supported filter names
filter_var()	filters a variable with a specified filter
filter_var_array()	gets multiple variables and filter them

PHP File Permission Chart

Number	Permission
0	cannot read, write or execute
1	can only execute
2	can only write
3	can write and execute
4	can only read
5	can read and execute
6	can read and write
7	can read, write and execute

PHP String Format Chart

Symbol	Represent
%%	percent sign
%b	binary number
%c	the character according to the ascii value
%d	signed decimal number (negative, zero or positive)
%e	scientific notation using a lowercase (e.g. 1.2e+2)
%E	scientific notation using a uppercase (e.g. 1.2e+2)
%u	unsigned decimal number (equal to or greater than 0)
%f	floating-point number (local settings aware)
%F	floating-point number (not local settings aware)
%g	shorter of %e and %f
%G	shorter of %e and %f
%o	octal number
%s	string
%x	hexadecimal number (lowercase letters)
%X	hexadecimal number (uppercase letters)

PHP Data & Time Format Chart

Format	Description	Example
a	'am' or 'pm' lowercase	pm
A	'AM' or 'PM' uppercase	PM
d	Day of month, a number with leading zeroes	18
D	Day of week (three letters)	Thu
F	Month name	January
h	Hour (12-hour format - leading zeroes)	11
H	Hour (24-hour format - leading zeroes)	23
g	Hour (12-hour format - no leading zeroes)	11
G	Hour (24-hour format - no leading zeroes)	23
i	Minutes (0 - 59)	23
j	Day of the month (no leading zeroes	18
l	Day of the week	Monday
L	Leap year ('1' for yes, '0' for no)	1
m	Month of year (number - leading zeroes)	1
M	Month of year (three letters)	May
n	Month of year (number - no leading zeroes)	3
s	Seconds of hour	18
U	Time stamp	968292368
y	Year (two digits)	08
Y	Year (four digits)	2006
z	Day of year (0 - 365)	206
Z	Offset in seconds from GMT	+5

PHP Data Type Chart

Type	Description
String	characters within double or single quotation.
Integer	numbers without decimal point.
Boolean	a value with true or false.
Float	numbers with decimal point.

mysqli_xxx_xxx ( ) Chart

mysqli_affected_row ( ) Returns the number of row affected by query	
mysqli_close ( ) Closes the connection with MySQL server	
mysqli_connect ( ) Creates an initial connection with MySQL server	
mysqli_create_db ( ) Creates a database on the MySQL server	
mysqli_data_seek ( ) Adjusts the result pointer to a random row in the results	
mysqli_db_query ( ) This function was deprecated in PHP 5.3.0	
mysqli_error ( ) Returns a string with the error description	
mysqli_fetch_array ( ) Return an indexed and associative array that contains rows of a table.	
mysqli_fetch_assoc ( ) Return an associative array that contains rows of a table.	
mysqli_fetch_row ( ) Return an indexed array that contains rows of a table.	
mysqli_free_result ( ) Clears the system memory associated with the result	
mysqli_get_server_info ( ) Returns a string with the MySQL server version	
mysqli_num_rows ( ) Returns the number of rows in the result set	
mysqli_query ( ) Submits a query to the database on the server	
mysqli_real_escape_string ( ) Escapes special characters in a string for MySQL	
mysqli_result ( ) Returns a string of one cell from a MySQL result set	
mysqli_select_db ( ) Selects the database to use by database name	

MySQL Database Commands Chart

Commands	Descriptions
CREATE DATABASE database-name	create database
USE database-name	use a database
SHOW database-name	show a database
DROP database-name	remove a database

MySQL Table Commands Chart

Commands	Descriptions
CREATE TABLE table-name	create table
SHOW TABLE	show all tables
DESCRIBE	show fields property
SHOW COLUMNS FROM table-name	show a field property
SHOW INDEX FROM table-name	list index field property
ALTER TABLE table-name	change data of a field
DROP TABLE table-name	remove a table
OPTIMIZE table-name	optimize a table

MySQL Operation Commands Chart

Commands	Descriptions
SELECT field FROM table WHERE condition	query data
INSERT INTO table (field) VALUES (value)	insert data
DELETE FROM table WHERE condition	delete data
UPDATE table SET field = value WHERE condition	update data
PEPLACE INTO table (field) VALUES (value)	replace data

MySQL Data Type Chart

Type	Depiction
int	An integer from -2147483648 to 2147483647
decimal	A floating point number from -999.99 to 999.99.
double	A decimal number with double precision.
date	A date with the format YYYY-MM-DD
time	A time with the format HH:MM:SS
datetime	A digit with the format YYYY-MM-DD HH:MM:SS.
year	A year with the YYYY format from 1901 to 2155
timestamp	An automatic date & time of an event occurred.
char()	A string with fixed length up to 255 with padding.
varchar()	A string with variable length up to 255 no padding.
text	A string with length up to 65535 characters
blob	A variable with binary type.
enum	A single string value in a list.
set	A multiple string value in a list.

MySQL Field Modifier Chart

Modifier	Descriptions
AUTO_INCREMENT	automatically generate a serial number
NUT NULL	cannot be empty value
NULL	can be empty value
UNIQUE	cannot not duplicate any entry
PRIMARY KEY	specify as a primary key
DEFAULT	specify a default value for a field
INDEX	specify an index field for table

MySQL System Function Chart

Functions	Returns
cast(v as type)	Return the converted data type
connection_id()	Return the connecting id of the server
database()	Return the name of the current database
if(expr,m,n)	If expr is true, return m. If false, return n.
ifnull(m,n)	If m is not null, return m, otherwise return n
nullif(m, n)	If m equals n, return null, otherwise return m
user()	Return the name of the current user
version()	Return the version number of the database
show processlist	Display the id, user, host, db, command……

MySQL Numeric Function Chart

Functions	Returns
abs(n)	absolute value of n
avg(field)	average value of a field
ceiling(n)	the closest integer above n
cos(n)	cosine of n
exp(n)	exponential value of n
floor(n)	the closest integer below n
max(field)	maximum value of a field
min(field)	minimum value of a field
mod(m, n)	remainder of m divided by n
pi()	3.141593
radians(n)	degrees n converted to radians
rand(n)	random number between 0 to 1.0
round(n)	the closest integer to n
sin(n)	sine of n
sqrt(n)	square root of n
tan(n)	tangent of n

MySQL Datetime Function Chart

Functions	Returns
current_date()	the current date
current_time()	the current time
current_timestamp()	the current date and time
date(date)	the date of the date. e.g. 2020-01-18
day(date)	the day of the date. e.g. 18
dayname(date)	day name of the date. e.g. Saturday
hour(date)	the hour of the date
minute(date)	the minute of the date
month(date)	the month of the date
monthname(date)	month name of the date. e.g. January
now()	the current date and time
second(date)	the second of the date
year(date)	the year of the date

MySQL Statement Chart

alter table TableName **add** FieldName type modifier;   (add a field)
alter table TableName **add primary key** (FieldName);   (add a primary key)
alter table TableName **add unique** (FieldName);   (set unique property for a field)
alter table TableName **alter** FieldName **set/drop default**;   (set or remove default value for a field)
alter table TableName **change** FieldName1 FieldName2;   (change field name)
alter table TableName **drop** FieldName;   (remove a field)
alter table TableName **drop** FieldName;   (remove a field)
alter table TableName **drop** primary key;   (remove the primary key)
alter table TableName **modify** FieldName type modifier;   (modify data type or modifier)
begin;   (start a transaction)
call ProcedureName;   (call the stored procedure)
commit;   (execute a transaction)
count (distinct FieldName)   (count the records with unique values in the specified field.)
count (FieldName)   (count the non-empty records in the field)
count(*)   (count all records in the table)
create database DatabaseName;   (create a new database)
create database if not exists DatabaseName;   (create a database)
create table if not exists NewTable   **select * from** OldTable;   (copy a whole table)
create table if not exists TableName (col1 type1, col2 type2);   (create a table)
create table TableName (col1 type1, col2 type2, col3 type3);   (create a table)

create view ViewName (FieldNames) **as select** statements; (create a view)
create view ViewName (FieldNames) **as select** statements; (alter a view)
delete from TableName **where** field = value; (delete a record)
delete from TableName **where** id = int; (remove a record)
delete from TableName; (delete all records)
describe TableName; (show the table format)
drop database DatabaseName; (remove a database)
drop database if exists DatabaseName; (remove a database)
drop procedure if exists ProcedureName; (remove a stored procedure)
drop table if exists TableName; (drop a table)
drop table TableName; (remove a table)
drop view if exists ViewName; (remove a view)
engine=innodb; (use innodb database engine)
explain TableName; (know about the table format)
FieldName **primary key,** (set a field as a primary key)
group by FieldName; (group data in the field)
having condition (filter the groups)
insert into TableName (field1, field2, field3) values (value1, value2, value3); (input data into a table)
order by field **asc;** (sort the data in ascending order)
order by field **desc;** (sort the data in descending order)
order by FieldName; (sort the data in a field)

rename table old_table_name **to** new_table_name; (rename a table) (change an old table name to a new table name)
rollback; (cancel a transaction)
select * from TableName; (show table data)
select @variable_name; (show the variable value)
select * from FieldName **as** alias; (set a field name)
select * from TableName **where** FieldName **between**…**and**… (show records in a certain range)
select * from TableName **where** FieldName **!=** value; (show records without a specified value)
select * from TableName **where** FieldName **less/more than** value; (show records less/more than a specified value)
select * from TableName **where** expression1 **and** expression2; (show records that satisfy two conditions.)
select * from TableName **where** expression1 **or** expression2; (show records that satisfy one of the conditions.)
select * from TableName **where** FieldName **in** (value1, value2, value3); (show records in an available range)
select * from TableName **where** FieldName **like** "%value%" (show records containing a similar value with some characters)
select * from TableName **where** FieldName **like** "_value_" (show records containing a similar value with one character)
select * from TableName **where** FieldName **regexp** pattern (show records whose value matches the specified pattern)
select * from TableName **order by rand()** **limit** n; (get random records)
select * from TableName **order by** FieldName; (show sorted data in a field)

select * from TableName **where** field = value; (show a specified record)	
select * from TableName1 **union all** **select * from** TableName2 **union all** **select * from** TableName3; (combine multiple select queries in one table)	
select @variable_name := value; (define a variable and show its value)	
select alias1.field1, alias2.field2 **from** table1 **as** alias1 **join** table2 **as** alias2 **on** alias1.fieldname = alias2.fieldname; (show two joined tables' data in one table)	
select alias1.field1, alias2.field2 **from** table1 **as** alias1 **left join** table2 **as** alias2 **on** alias1.fieldname = alias2.fieldname; (show two joined tables' data, including complete left-table data)	
select alias1.field1, alias2.field2 **from** table1 **as** alias1 **right join** table2 **as** alias2 **on** alias1.fieldname = alias2.fieldname; (show two joined tables' data, including complete right-table data)	
select concat(field1, "separator" , field2) **from** TableName; (connect two or more fields together)	
select count(*) **from** TableName; (count all records in the table)	
select count(**distinct** FieldName) **from** TableName; (show the records with unique values in the specified field.)	
select count(FieldName) **from** TableName; (count the non-empty records in the field)	
select distinct FieldName **from** TableName; (show the records with unique values in the specified field)	
select Field, **count(*) from** Table **group by** Field; (show the data grouped by fields)	
select Field1, Field2, Field3 **from** table1, table2, table3; (show multiple tables in one table)	
select field1, field2, field3 **from** TableName; (show specified fields)	
select sum(FieldName) **from** TableName;. (sum up the value of the specified field)	
set @variable_name := value; (define a variable)	
set autocommit=0; (disable autocommit)	

set autocommit=1; (enable autocommit)	
show databases; (show all existing databases)	
show tables; (show all the existing tables)	

stored procedure;
 delimiter //
   create procedure ProcedureName()
     begin
       select statement;
     end //
 delimiter;	

table1 **join** table2 (join table1 and table2)	
table1 **left join** table2 (join two table's data, including complete left-table data)	
table1 **right join** table2 (join two table's data, including complete right-table data)	
update TableName **set** field1 = value1, field2 = value2 where field = value; (update fields)	
update TableName **set** FieldName = value; (update the data for all records in a field)	
update TableName **set** FieldName = value; (update the data for a specified record in a field)	
use DatabaseName; (select a database)	
where condition (filter the records)	

Cheat Sheet by Ray Yao

C# Cheat Sheet   Php MySql Cheat Sheet
C++ Cheat Sheet   Python Cheat Sheet
Java Cheat Sheet   Html Css Cheat Sheet
JavaScript Cheat Sheet   Linux Command Line

Made in the USA
Middletown, DE
24 April 2024